Setting
the
Agenda

"A unique and inspired work that boldly and unabashedly invites board members to act in a caring and spiritual way as they serve organizations. This book will be of special interest to board trustees."
—Larry C. Spears, author of *The Spirit of Servant-Leadership* and president of The Spears Center for Servant-Leadership

"Stoesz and Stiffney provide a powerful and accessible argument that a board of directors is more than the sum of its resolutions. The practical advice of the authors is amplified by the inspiring and sometimes sobering real-life anecdotes in the second section."
—Art DeFehr, president and CEO of Palliser Furniture

"Stoesz and Stiffney help us step back and see the board as a whole, asking us to also pay attention to the organization's soul. The principles spoken to and the wealth of devotional material will serve boards well."
—Kenneth Hoke, executive director of International Brethren in Christ Association and owner of KOH Coaching & Consulting

Setting
the
Agenda

Meditations
for the
Organization's
Soul

Edgar Stoesz and Rick M. Stiffney

Foreword by Margaret Benefiel

Herald Press

Scottdale, Pennsylvania
Waterloo, Ontario

LIBRARY OF CONGRESS CATALOGING-PUBLICATION-DATA
Stoesz, Edgar.
  Setting the agenda : meditations for the organization's soul / Edgar
Stoesz and Rick M. Stiffney ; foreword by Margaret Benefiel.
     p. cm.
  Includes bibliographical references (p.   ) and index.
  ISBN 978-0-8361-9556-9 (pbk.)
   1. Religious institutions—Management. 2. Religious institutions—
Employees—Prayers and devotions. I. Stiffney, Rick M., 1951- II. Title.
  BV900.S76 2011
  250—dc22
                                                 2011000876

SETTING THE AGENDA
Copyright @ 2011 by Herald Press, Scottdale, Pennsylvania 15683
  Released simultaneously in Canada by Herald Press,
  Waterloo, Ont. N2L 6H7. All rights reserved.
Library of Congress Control Number: 2011000876
International Standard Book Number: 978-0-8361-9556-9
Printed in United States of America
Cover by Reuben Graham

16 15 14 13 12 11   10 9 8 7 6 5 4 3 2 1

To order or request information please call
1-800-245-7894 or visit www.heraldpress.com.

*We dedicate this book to the many individuals
with whom we've interacted and
the organizations that have shaped
our vision for board service that is more effective,
more God honoring, and more fulfilling.*

Contents

Foreword

"We are all people of faith, on the board of a faith-based organization, yet we rarely acknowledge God's presence in our midst, let alone ask God for help." So spoke a competent, successful, faithful board member in a conversation in which I participated last night. As we reflected on the challenges that lay before the board in question, the board member bemoaned the lack of spirituality in the board's meetings. Not only that, but even worse, he mentioned the apparently inverse correlation between, on the one hand, competence and worldly success in a board member and, on the other hand, willingness to turn to God in the midst of board deliberations.

If such conversations were uncommon, *Setting the Agenda* would not be needed. Unfortunately, the board member's complaint represents a refrain I hear again and again. Why is it that the minute a faith-based board gets down to its "real business," the faith base crumbles? Why does the inverse correlation between worldly success and willingness to turn to God so often hold? What would it take for a faith-based board to take its faith seriously and build its meetings on a spiritual foundation? How can the board of a faith-based organization incorporate spirituality into its meetings when it is an ecumenical, perhaps even interfaith, board?

While national debates about faith-based organizations, their place in a society that is committed to separation of church and state, and their relationship to federal and state funding continue, one conversation that rarely occurs is the one about how a faith base becomes operationalized. If faith-based organizations constitute an integral part of American society, they need to learn to put their faith into action in their governance, so that they can fully live out their mission.

Setting the Agenda, written and edited by two practitioners who understand these issues intimately, provides practical help for any board members who have ever asked themselves these questions and felt frustrated. Edgar Stoesz, author of *Doing Good Even Better* and *Meditations for Meetings*, and Rick Stiffney, national Mennonite Health Services Alliance executive and consultant to many boards, both have extensive firsthand experience with the governance of faith-based organizations.

Part 1 sets the stage by considering why and how spirituality can be integrated into organizational life. These chapters help kindle vision in board members for how spirituality can be expressed in organizations, for who can help foster it, and for how it can be fostered.

Part 2 provides a wealth of practical resources for spiritually minded board members by introducing various topics useful for devotional focus in board meetings and then offering nearly a hundred meditations. The meditations, written by different authors serving in the trenches, provide a reflective, prayerful focus to open and/or close meetings and to help orient boards to their purpose and vision as they commence and close their business.

Setting the Agenda offers an important contribution to the literature on faith-based not-for-profits. By venturing into the largely uncharted territory of spirituality and board leadership, Stiffney and Stoesz have proved themselves courageous and groundbreaking pioneers. May board members of faith-based organizations take these words to heart and experiment with the meditations. My hunch is that, if they do, they will see their organizations transformed.

Margaret Benefiel
Author of Soul at Work *and*
The Soul of a Leader
December 2010

Preface

Writing and editing this book has been an epiphany for us. We hope readers will also find it a high moment of inspiration. We prepared it for board members looking for new sources of wisdom and power, both in their private and public service lives. In turn, we believe they can make their board service more effective and fulfilling.

Our search of the available literature reveals an abundance of books on personal spirituality, some of them quite good. Although spirituality in the workplace has received considerable interest, little attention has been given to spirituality in the boardroom, particularly the soul of nonprofit organizations. This silence is surprising because many organizations are in or come out of the faith-based tradition.

This book is made up of two parts. Part 1 is a philosophical discussion on why and how spirituality already is or can more fully become part of an organization's soul. We assert that the spirituality of an organization and its leaders shapes the organization and all that it does. Then we discuss who is responsible to foster it and how. We offer pathways into the heart and soul for spirit-led service. Attention to spirituality is not a retreat from daily responsibilities but is attending to the moving of God's Spirit in our midst.

Part 2 contains ninety-five meditations that board members may use in the boardroom, divided into six chapters that represent the moods and challenges that boards face. Each chapter includes a short discussion of the topic and offers prayers that leaders may choose to use or adapt for their use.

We offer this book in the spirit of the apostle Paul, who in writing to the Philippians (3:12) says, "Not that I have already obtained this or have already reached the goal; but I press on to make it my own, because Christ has made me his own."

Now we invite you to read *Setting the Agenda* with an open and receptive mind, allowing the Spirit to show you its application in your life and in the life of the organization you represent.

Edgar Stoesz
Rick Stiffney
October 1, 2010

Acknowledgments

We express profound gratitude to the writers of these meditations. They are an impressive body of writers who willingly shared out of the wealth of their spirituality and boardroom experience.

We offer our gratitude to Amy Gingerich and Levi Miller and others, including graphic artists at the Mennonite Publishing Network, for putting our efforts into an attractive and readable book and making it available through its wide distribution system.

We give our gratitude to the MHS Alliance staff who assisted with the collection and management of this material.

Finally, special mention is deservedly due Mim Shirk, vice president with Mennonite Health Services Alliance, who was an active participant and guide throughout the entire process.

Part 1

Setting an Agenda for Boardroom Spirituality

1

Discovering Spirituality: The Missing Piece

We hear it from many of the organizational leaders we meet—a deep longing within the soul. Our busy lives exact a high price from us. Our systems of government, our powerful corporations, our agencies of compassion, even our churches (some say especially our churches) are under heavy strain. Even the adoption of best practices takes us only so far. "The world we have made as a result of the thinking we have done thus far," said Albert Einstein, "is creating problems that cannot be solved at the level we have created them" (paraphrased).

An Indian poet described it with these words: "The song I came to sing is unsung. I spent my life stringing and unstringing my instrument." On bad days we feel like Pogo, who concluded, "We have met the enemy and it is us." These longings were addressed by the apostle Paul:

> So we do not lose heart. Even though our outer nature is wasting away, our inner nature is being renewed day by day. For this slight momentary affliction is preparing us for an eternal weight of glory beyond all measure, *because we look not at what can be seen but at what cannot be seen; for what can be seen is temporary, but what cannot be seen is eternal.* (2 Cor 4:16-18, emphasis added)

What we see is temporary: legal charters, reams of minutes, agendas, and meeting dockets with carefully prepared reports will all pass away. The landscape is littered with the remains of well-

21

intended organizations. Like the flowers of the field in the Bible's imagery, they flourish for a time, then wither and die, leaving little to remember. Several of the top performing companies Jim Collins featured in his much-lauded book *Good to Great* have in only a few years fallen on hard times. Only that which cannot be seen is eternal.

In the poem "In Memoriam," the poet Alfred Lord Tennyson says:

> Our little systems have their day;
>> They have their day and cease to be:
>> They are but broken lights of thee,
> And thou, O Lord, art more than they.

> We have but faith; we cannot know:
>> For knowledge is of things we see;
>> And yet we trust it comes from thee,
> A beam in darkness: let it grow.[1]

Robert Greenleaf, the Quaker former AT&T executive and servanthood leadership advocate, says, "The leader needs two intellectual abilities that are not usually assessed in an academic way: the leader needs to have *a sense for the unknowable* and be able to *foresee the unforeseeable*."[2] Leaders who develop their intuition and draw on invisible spiritual resources are needed.

Margaret Benefiel, in *Soul at Work*, a book committed to increasing congruence between spiritual values and work, explicitly declares that half of our managerial decisions fail. They fail because they are fixated on the present and do not know how to anticipate the future. They fail because directors read and base their decisions on what is on the lines. Spiritual insights are required to read what is between the lines.

The solutions to organizational problems come from the soul, say Eric Klein and John Izzo in *Awakening Corporate Soul*. They suggest that organizational leaders need to do more than fixate on the balance sheet, on team building, or on annual work plans. Their solution is to create an environment that feeds the soul.[3]

William A. Guillory, in *The Living Organization*, also suggests what others have discovered: "Spirituality is a life force that permeates and drives a living organization in the pursuit of its objectives."[4]

Yet words like *spiritual*, *sacred*, or *soul* are not found in most organizational lexicons. As directors, we are a confident bunch: we believe in ourselves. Spirituality, many think, is inappropriate in a boardroom. But against expectations, might it turn out to be the missing piece? Might soul be at the heart of what is eluding so many of us?

The Many Expressions of Spirituality

Before launching into an abbreviated survey of the rich and diverse literature of humankind's search for a spirituality that sustains and gives meaning to life, we need to correct a common misconception. Spirituality is not to be confused with religion. *Spirituality* is essence. *Religion* is form. Religion is only one of the many forms through which spirituality is expressed. Through the Spirit, humans are able to transcend the physical world that surrounds us and experience the transcendent.

We have a number of languages of the soul. Lovers of music, art, and nature enter another world, rich with mystery and the unknown. A friend describes taking a photo of a flower in all its splendor as a spiritual experience.

Catholic spirituality has a long history of recognizing the importance of contemplation. In the twelfth century, Francis of Assisi wrote the famous prayer, "Lord, make me an instrument of your peace." In the fifteenth century we connect with Ignatius of Loyola, who authored five major works on spirituality before Christopher Columbus's famous 1492 voyage. Later John of the Cross in his book identified *The Dark Night of the Soul*. Coming to the modern period, Thomas Merton (1915–68) authored 70 books, the best known being *The Seven Storey Mountain*. Finally, Henri J. M. Nouwen (1932–96) published 40 books, including *Return of the Prodigal Son*.

Quaker spirituality dates back to 1652, when George Fox founded the Society of Friends. Fox and his contemporaries were so moved by the Spirit that their bodies "quaked," giving them their nickname. Quaker spirituality seeks to be in tune with the inner life found in silence, in the Bible, and in listening to each other. Quakers believe intently that there is "that of God" in everyone. The Quaker practice of discernment honors this belief.

The Celtic way of prayer has inspired many Christians. Life is seen as a whole, making no distinction between the sacred and the secular. Celtic prayer takes a natural and conversational approach. The Trinity (God, Jesus, and the Holy Spirit) is recognized as being present in each moment. Prayer blesses everything in life, except evil.

Mennonite scholar J. Nelson Kraybill describes spirituality within the Anabaptist faith tradition as Jesus-centered and rooted in the Scriptures. Its emphasis is on a vigorous inner life, along with a commitment to holy living, justice, truth-telling, and non-violence.

Eastern religions, particularly Buddhism, have given much attention to their spirituality. Buddhism has become popularized by the much-honored Nobel Peace Prize-winning (1989) Dalai Lama XIV, also known as the President of the Tibetan government-in-exile.

Our stance in this book is to respect and receive insight from all spiritual traditions that create a greater awareness of God's presence, although we subscribe to a spirituality that is based on the teachings and life of Jesus as portrayed in the Bible.

How Spirituality Is Expressed in a Faith-Affiliated Organization

Though spirituality can be found in both secular and faith-affiliated settings, our focus in this book is addressed in a particular way (though not exclusively) to organizations with a faith orientation. Prominent among them is the church itself.

From its beginning, as recorded in the book of Acts, the church has viewed ministering to the needy as an essential part of its Christian and civic duty. The value of services rendered daily by congregations in their respective communities cannot be quantified. It is a valuable part of society's safety net for the poor and disenfranchised.

In addition, the church has birthed an array of social-service organizations such as the Salvation Army, Church World Service, Catholic Relief Services, and myriad local and regional organizations. Denominationally sponsored ministries are often legally linked to their parent body through bylaw provisions, including the prerogative to appoint members to their governing board.

While parachurch organizations have activities and characteristics similar to denominationally sponsored ministries, their support comes from across the denominational spectrum. They do not have a legal or structural relationship to a specific church body. Examples are World Vision and Habitat for Humanity International.

Collectively these church-related bodies have come to be known as faith-based organizations. We can summarize their unique contribution in three categories:

> Urgently needed is a written theology of institutions. David Specht and Richard Broholm have made a good beginning in a paper "Toward a Theology of Institutions," available from the Greenleaf Center.[5]

1. *An ethic of compassion.* The foundational ethic of love of neighbor has its basis in both Old and New Testament texts such as Leviticus 19:18 and Matthew 22:34-40. The injunction to help the poor and needy is not seen as optional; the Christian's salvation is predicated on it (1 John 3:17). Through this personal involvement, the church has a continuing presence in these communities and places of conflict.

The bedrock of all ministries of compassion is stated in what is known as the fruit of the spirit, as listed in Galatians 5:22-23. They are "love, joy, peace, patience, kindness, generosity, faithfulness, gentleness, and self control." Finally, biblical injunctions go to the root of human need by advocating justice and creation care.

We acknowledge parenthetically that the church is enriching its own soul by participating in these ministries. This makes it a reciprocal relationship, but not one free from challenges. By attending to the wounded at the side of the road, some fear the church is becoming distracted from evangelism or gathering into fellowships, both of which some see as the church's main function. On the other extreme are those who fear that the church is too sectarian in the performance of its social welfare role. The tension is probably inherent and inevitable.

2. *Institutional grounding.* Jack Shea, a well-known Catholic ethicist and an expert on nonprofit governance, warns that over time many nonprofits become disaffiliated from the community

of faith and become devoid of any faith meaning. Through a formal relationship, a church-related nonprofit organization is more likely to retain the faith perspectives and the values of the founders and resist being co-opted by only the secular environments within which it is situated. Sometimes these dynamics are even accelerated by changes in board membership or by employing a CEO who does not prize an ongoing relationship to a church body or does not embody the core values of the community of faith.

3. *Increasing the quantum of aid.* The social-welfare contribution of the churches in such fields as health (including recently AIDS/HIV sufferers), education, care for the elderly, youth, camps, addiction, and on and on is inestimable. Contributions to faith-based organizations run well into the hundreds of millions of dollars annually. An even larger contribution may be in the value of volunteer services.

The missing piece for many boards is the conscious recognition, the deliberate drawing in, of the Spirit. This transforming and enabling resource is freely available. All that boards need to do is acknowledge it and make room for it.

2

Moving Spirituality: From Periphery to Pervasive

Boards vary in how, or even if, faith is consciously incorporated into their deliberations. Some, and this includes some faith-based organizations, have no overt awareness of the transcendent, although the directors themselves may be deeply religious. One person calls these boards "quietly agnostic."

Some boards open and close their meetings with a moment of silence or a short prayer, sometimes with a short meditation thrown in. They may use biblical language in their mission and values statements while their agendas are packed with routine business. They hear reports, approve budgets and work plans, but with little reference to the metrics of faith. Still other boards seek to conduct meetings with a conscious sense of God's presence from gavel to adjournment. The whole meeting is conducted in an awareness of the transcendent. This is illustrated in the following graphic on page 28.

Levels of Conscious Spirituality in Board Meetings

1. Conscious, overt spirituality is limited to a moment of silence to start the meeting. Beyond that the directors draw on their own wisdom and experience to make wise decisions.

2. The opening invocation is expanded to include a brief mediation, including a Scripture reading, perhaps a reading from a meditation book (like this one), and a spoken prayer. Then the focus shifts to the prepared agenda: the business of the meeting.

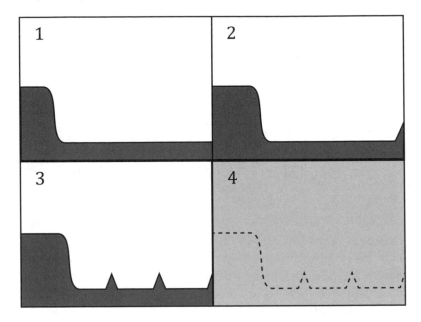

3. The meeting opens with a meditation as in stage 2 but additionally the board pauses at strategic times to pray or reflect before making a major decision. The meeting closes with a brief prayer.

4. The entire meeting takes place against the background of a conscious sense of God's presence, with the transition to the working agenda barely visible. The meeting concludes with a time of reflection, including a prayer asking God to guide the implementation of the decisions made.

Humans never master this world of the Spirit; they are unable to think their way into it. Deliberate thought may prove to be a distraction. It is more appropriate for directors to think in terms of making room for the Spirit, of giving ourselves over to the Spirit.

Living in this world of the Spirit is not an activity that can be scheduled by hour or minutes. Spirituality is not a department within the organization. Spirituality in the boardroom is in being, along with doing. It informs what boards do and, more important, how they do it. Humans are more likely to experience this world when they have exhausted their intelligence and allow themselves to enter the world of unknowing, where the peace of God "surpasses all understanding" (Phil 4:7).

How Spirituality Express Itself

Governance is not an academic exercise. Boards have a fiduciary responsibility to perform tangible services in behalf of their members: to deliver results, to change lives. To that end governing boards routinely approve budgets and establish annual and long-range plans. They identify key performance indicators and delegate responsibility.

So what, action-minded directors ask, is the role of spirituality in that process? How is faith integrated with the work of governance?

The simple truth is that achieving a higher level of spiritual consciousness requires a new mind-set, a new way of thinking. Old ways of thinking will produce only more of the same. We offer the following practical suggestions:

1. *Spirituality helps directors see themselves as stewards, not owners.* The Scriptures remind us that in Christ "all things in heaven and on earth were created, things visible and invisible, whether thrones or dominions or rulers or powers—all things have been created through him and for him. . . . In [Christ] all things hold together" (Col 1:16-17).

The organizations to which directors give such loving care do not belong to them. The whole works belongs to God, who dwells in Christ. Directors who are responsible to run these organizations are caretakers, not owners. This reminder helps directors to see their role more correctly as stewards in God's vineyard, not masters of a private fiefdom. It is well stated in a hymn:

> At a board retreat, the board chair asked that all of the planning work be viewed from the vantage of trustees seeing themselves as stewards of opportunities and resources entrusted to them. Although simple, this reminder was profound in its consequence. Over the ensuing hours, board members without provocation returned to the theme of stewardship to reflect on how being a trustee of someone else's work should inform the process.

> The work is Thine, O Christ our Lord,
> The cause for which we stand,
> And being Thine, 'twill overcome
> Its foes on ev'ry hand.[1]

2. *Spirituality helps provide an alternate frame of reference.* Many boards—we are tempted to say most boards—operate with a false sense of self-sufficiency and well-being. Their thinking and planning horizons are short, and their understanding of their role is inadequate. Better organizational performance begins with better governance, and better governance begins with seeing things whole.[2]

If directors can understand only what they can see, they are only seeing the half. Directors need to lift themselves out of the present to peer into the future—and that is a spiritual exercise!

The powerful words of Eckhart Tolle poignantly present this challenge:

> A large multisite organization with roots in an evangelical religious tradition had grown to serve a pluralistic marketplace with a diverse workforce. Board and senior leadership agreed that it was important to revisit their core mission and sense of identity. They were led away from operational issues and refocused on what it means to be faithful to the core convictions of the founding community of faith while serving many different communities of need.

Is humanity ready for a transformation of consciousness, an inner flowering so radical and profound that compared to it the flowering of plants, no matter how beautiful, is only a pale reflection? Can human beings lose the density of their conditioned mind structures and become like crystals or precious stones, so to speak, transparent to the light of consciousness? Can they defy the gravitational pull of materialism and materiality and rise above identification with form that keeps the ego in place and condemns them to imprisonment within their own personality?[3]

3. *Spirituality helps boards ask difficult questions.* Good governance is as much about asking the right question as about offering the right answers. A board that is spiritually strong finds it easier to cultivate a culture of inquiry. The ability to ask good, analytical questions distinguishes a great board from an ordinary board.

Instead of obsessing over operational issues, which in any case are in the domain of the CEO, governing boards engage in what has been called "generative work." Ask: How do our mission and values inform this decision? What have we learned? What are the possibilities? Generative work moves us as directors back to mission and forward toward the future. Generative work deals with matters that really matter.[4]

4. *Spirituality helps nurture changes in attitudes.* A climate of conscious spirituality in the boardroom changes how directors go about their work, how they address each other, and how they view the future. Much conflict in the boardroom results from out-of-control egos. Ego and spirituality do not co-exist well. Ego is concerned first about self and has little room for the supernatural or collaborative decision making, the hallmark of a great board.

Servant directors are gentle and thoughtful in their dealings. They are slow to point the accusing finger. They put the interests of others and the cause ahead of themselves. Instead of jockeying for high office or building a personal resume, their whole orientation is that of servants. They embrace mystery; dependence on the Spirit replaces an attitude of arrogance. Kingdom building replaces empire building.

The best posture for directors of a faith-based organization is to see themselves as being within and under God's rule. This should not be understood as an escape from the hard reality in which most nonprofits operate. To the contrary, it should inspire directors to do no less than their best for the cause, guided of the Holy Spirit. Instead of being consumed by internal conflicts, they have the inner strength to confront difficult issues and address new challenges courageously while being open to new ways of thinking.

> A large denomination was giving thought to expanding into the international scene to increase its identity. In a thoughtful strategic planning session, the question of board composition arose. They agreed that it was important to emphasize their denominational core convictions and that the governing board should be composed of persons who professed Christian faith. This caused a member to resign since he did not profess faith, although he supported the restriction. This kind of conversation is spirituality in the boardroom.

A spiritually strong board works in an atmosphere of mutual respect. Directors value each other's opinions. They listen well. They welcome differing points of view. Some have even suggested that boards adopt a "dissent agenda"—a set of issues about which they know there can and should be lively disagreement in the boardroom. Board chairs make an effort to elicit thoughtful comment from all board members, not only those who are habitually first to respond. Their decision-making ideal is consensus, and when that is not possible, they differ with each other respectfully. This sometimes takes longer but results in more-enduring decisions. The goal is to integrate spirituality with the pragmatics of board work.

> Board dynamics can be like making a good cup of tea. If the tea bag is removed after the water has reached a certain color, only the quick-releasing elements will have acted. The best tea occurs after the slow-releasing elements have been allowed to contribute to the taste.

Spirituality is not some esoteric, amorphous theory that academicians banter around in a classroom. It is not a substitute for the best board practices. The stance we advocate is not pray or plan, but pray and plan. William Guillory summarizes it well when he describes how organizations are at their best when spiritual principles are combined with sound business practices.[5]

Who Takes Responsibility?

The spirituality of an organization resides with its people, beginning with the directors and senior management, and finally it resides with everyone within the organization. Without the human element, organizations are but an empty shell. Organizations are what people create with them: people own them, run them, and are served by them.

"It is easier," says Parker Palmer in his book *Leading from Within*, "to spend your life manipulating an institution than to deal with your own soul."[6] Directors set the tone for the entire organization. Only when directors operate with a sense of God in their personal lives and board service can they expect that from their employees. It is simply not possible for an organization to be more spiritual than the people who lead it. It is necessary for boards and chief executives to keep this in mind as they plan for and conduct meetings, select new board members, and plan board orientation and enrichment activities.

But it is not as simple as saying that the values of the organization are a composite of the values of the people in them. In the first place, not all directors have a defined sense of their own spirituality. Even directors who practice spirituality in their private lives often check their personal values at the boardroom door, and to get along with others, they move with the prevailing majority. Additionally there is the danger that in arriving at a consensus, the lowest common denominator prevails instead of inspiring each other to a deeper spirituality.

> A college board we know finds it hard to cover its operating expenses from student fees. In struggling with the issue of deficits, the board has learned three important things about governance. First, the board and the president need a high level of trust. Second, the board needs to muscle-up the courage to challenge the president and leadership team, setting the parameters within which administration can operate. Finally, the board must stay vigilant on issues of organizational ethos that may jeopardize the future. Board members have learned to speak forthrightly. All members are expected to engage in the discussion that leads up to a decision. One board member has been assigned to be particularly attentive to moments when a spoken prayer might be appropriate. Business and faith are intertwined.

Finally, we cannot overlook the role the CEO and senior staff have in modeling spirituality every day. CEOs have an enormous influence over shaping the board agenda and in setting the tone for the decision-making process. They transmit their spirituality through how they approach decision making and in how they treat others. The spirituality that is practiced by the board is transmitted through the members and permeates the entire organization.

3

Achieving Spirituality: Some Practical Suggestions

We now move to practical questions of how to apply all this fine-sounding theory in the boardroom. Directing a nonprofit organization is after all not an academic exercise. It involves wrestling with really knotty dilemmas and risk-taking challenges.

The journey—and it is a journey—begins logically by more consciously acknowledging and drawing on the Holy Spirit. Before departing into heaven Jesus promised his disciples unequivocally, "You will receive power when the Holy Spirit has come upon you" (Acts 1:8). The Holy Spirit can be the ladder to access that hallowed place of the Spirit beyond human reach. Lacking too often are the receptors to receive the artesian powers of the Spirit waiting to be utilized.

Five Practical Suggestions

We offer five practical suggestions for leaders who want to heighten their awareness of God in board deliberations. In the course of doing so, additional ways will no doubt be discovered.

1. *Make spirituality a serious priority.* It begins with a sincere recognition of the need. Some hesitate to invite the subject of spirituality onto our board agenda because we feel awkward about it. We don't know how to get started. We fear becoming bogged down in theological or denominational disputes. Like so much in life, the practice of spirituality must be learned. It won't happen by itself. No one can require a board to do it, nor can anyone do it for them. It is not covered in most organizational manuals. This book

> Spiritual growth can be likened to seeing in the dark. At first a room may appear to be altogether dark. As the eye adjusts, it begins to see a beam of light invading the room, or the faint outlines of an object. After a while it is possible to move around in the room cautiously. Eventually, in the words of poet Theodore Roethke, "In a dark time, the eye begins to see."[1] The light is not as bright as noonday, but it increases as one learns to work in it.

will, we hope, be a tipping point for many boards to make a new beginning. From that point the Spirit will guide you. It can be an epiphany, as writing this book was for us!

2. *Pray in new ways*. Prayer has been called the breath of the soul. Thérèse of Lisieux calls prayer "the surge of the heart, . . . something supernatural that engages my soul and unites it with God."[2]

Discovering a meaningful prayer life can be as hard as it is basic. Like the disciples, we call on Jesus to teach us how to pray meaningfully. We take comfort and find direction in the words of the apostle Paul:

> Likewise the Spirit helps us in our weakness; for we do not know how to pray as we ought, but that very Spirit intercedes with sighs too deep for words. And God, who searches the heart, knows what is the mind of the Spirit, because the Spirit intercedes for the saints according to the will of God. (Rom 8:26-27)

Organizational leaders need to learn how to present their petitions in prayer. Prayer need not consist of the "holy language" many are used to hearing in church. Walter Wink, in *Engaging the Powers*, says prayer is "impertinent, persistent, shameless, and indecorous. It is more like haggling in an outdoor bazaar than the polite monologues of the churches."[3] The point is this: the intent of prayer is far more important than the form or the words. Just as in our personal lives, sometimes the complexity of the challenge being addressed is just too big for words. It may be that mumbling together is more profound than the most eloquent of prayers.

In his book *Prayer*, Richard Foster similarly suggests that we should present our needs unapologetically: "Like Abraham we bargain with God over the fate of the city (Gen 18). Like Moses we argue with God over the fate of the people (Exod

32). Like Esther we plead with God over the fate of the nation (Esther 4)."[4]

Prayer does two things: It aligns us with God and puts us in a position where we can receive God's blessing and guidance. It reflects our dependence on a power or a source that is within and/ or beyond us. It is a posture of humble service and vulnerability. In prayer we invite God to be the center and guiding principle of life, as stated so beautifully in a hymn, "We give thee but thine own, whate'er the gift may be. All that we have is thine alone, a trust, O Lord, from thee."[5]

"The prayer of the righteous is powerful and effective," says the epistle of James (5:16). Through prayer, organizational leaders experience inner renewal, or else they find themselves running on empty. In prayer, leaders find direction and strength to carry on through good times and bad. A transcendental relationship through prayer adds soul and integrity to our work.

3. *See God in the ordinary*. Ronald Rolheiser, in *The Shattered Lantern*, decries what he calls "the eclipse of God in ordinary awareness."[6] Much of what nonprofits do, such as caring for the poor, is actually kingdom work: it needs to be recognized as such and done in that spirit. Often what is lacking also in faith-based organizations is recognition that God is already present and acting in the ordinary events of our lives and in the organizations we lead.

This effort is wonderfully illustrated in the little classic featuring Brother Lawrence, a seventeenth-century monk who thought he was being called to a position of responsibility in the monastery. Upon arriving, he found himself relegated to kitchen duty. Yet among the pots and pans he was so genuine in practicing the presence of God that the monks came to learn from him.[7]

Mennonite Health Services Alliance has developed an instrument for faith-based nonprofit boards to assess the degree to which certain practices of spiritual vitality are evidenced in the boardroom. Although leaders may differ over what indicators should be used to assess the level of board spirituality, the exercise helps to elevate the importance of this dimension.

With Jacob after hearing God's promises in a dream, we say, "Surely the Lord is in this place, and we knew it not" (cf. Gen 28:16). The boardroom as much as the chapel can be home for the Spirit.

Raising spirituality to a more-conscious level within the organization requires time, not a budget. We must make room for the Spirit to move in our midst. God does not force the Spirit on us. The Spirit does not interrupt a meeting to say, "Let me in. I have something to say."

Some boards appoint a member to serve as a kind of a listener for the Spirit! This person is expected to be especially alert for times when an epiphany moment is waiting to break in on them.

4. *Make room on the agenda.* Many boards are frustrated over too-long agendas and meetings. Much board work takes place in a hurried atmosphere, where Spirit-led discernment is precluded. Directors need to go beyond good intentions and arrange their agendas with space for the Spirit to move.

Boards generally conform to Robert's Rules of Order. These rules have their place. Order there must be, and the larger the assembly the more prescriptive the rules must be. But Robert's Rules clearly will not remind a board of the need to look anywhere but within itself.

Spirituality means seeing silence in a new light. Many boards assume subconsciously that time is well used only when someone is talking. Silence is regarded as a waste of time. Twice wrong! In an eternal sense, much of what passes for discussion is little more than empty blather. Silent contemplation may actually be golden. Pauses may be the holy space where human limitations are recognized and Spirit-led wisdom can flourish.

> A board chair asked each member to take a slip of paper from an envelope. On each paper was written a word from the organization's vision statement. In turn, members read the word on their paper, followed by a moment of quiet thought. It was a graphic reminder of what the board was aspiring to be and achieve.

"The soul speaks its truth only," says Parker Palmer, "under quiet, inviting, and trustworthy conditions. It is a silence that forever invites us to fathom the meaning of our lives—and forever reminds us of the depth of meaning that words cannot touch."[8] This applies as much to leaders personally as to board deliberations.

Making room for the Spirit helps a board to work smarter. Some discover that they are too busy *not* to pray! A question that may on the surface appear to have little relevance may lead to unanticipated discoveries that have powerful application. True spiritual consciousness is more likely to increase as directors come to the end of their human wisdom and open themselves to a new consciousness of God.

Spiritual directors refer to what they call the *susurrations* of God. By that they mean the gentle rustlings of the Spirit of God. Sometimes the work of the Spirit is like a mighty rushing wind. At other times it is almost imperceptible. Governing boards need to attend to the quiet ways as well as the more-dramatic ways in which the Spirit is at work.

5. *Expect surprises.* As stated so poignantly in a hymn by William Cowper (1774), "God works in a mysterious way, [God's] wonders to perform." God's ways are higher than our ways. Sometimes a new innovation that to our human way of thinking appears to be a no-brainer turns out to be a disaster, whereas what appears to be a crazy idea turns out to be transformative. Sometimes board work is analogous to Jesus' disciples, who had fished all night and caught nothing. Then Jesus came along and suggested that they try the other side of the boat, and the catch was so big it broke their nets! (Luke 5:1-11).

A large national board was engaged in the recruitment of a new executive director. A search committee had done extensive background work and interviewed several candidates. One candidate was brought back for a second interview, with the board anticipating that even if it went well, a third interview would be needed. Since the second interview went so well, the committee concluded that a third interview was not needed. After prayer, the committee invited the candidate, and he accepted the appointment. Both the candidate and the board were genuinely surprised by the clarity that came to them as they communicated with each other, waited in prayer, and arrived at a decision.

Though the working of the Spirit is beyond human perception, the Spirit is more than mystery. The Spirit can be a practical reality, available to help directors with their governance work. Sometimes the Spirit comes in subtle forms that are not recognizable and when we least expect it, but the Spirit is always there to guide us as we try to be good stewards of that which God has entrusted to our care.

4

Living Spirituality: Recognizing the Hills and Valleys

Living with greater spiritual awareness is not a flatland experience, however much we might wish it were. Whether in our private lives or in our official governance capacity, life with the Spirit (as in everything else!) has its ups and downs. At times we have a keen sense of God's leading in our little worlds. At other times God seems very distant and prayers seem like an exercise in futility. We are most likely to abandon prayer when we need it most.

Take heart. At Jesus' baptism a voice came from heaven: "You are my Son, the Beloved; with you I am well pleased" (Luke 1:22). What a wonderful affirmation. Three years later, when Jesus was hanging on the cross, he cried out, "My God, my God, why have you forsaken me" (Matt 27:46). Jesus felt forsaken by God, who had sent him on this difficult mission.

During the three years between this high and low, Jesus had other ups and downs. Many times the Gospels tell of Jesus being in direct communication with God.[1] Along the way he led a relatively ordinary life, yet he also was intense in serving God's will and ministering to others. He served as a carpenter, kept company with fishermen, and was entertained by the likes of Mary and Martha. On at least one occasion he became angry. He enjoyed bantering with the Pharisees. He advocated for a woman of bad reputation. Jesus, like us, had times when he felt close to God and other times when his life was very human.

A careful reading of the Psalms reveals the roller-coaster nature of King David's spiritual life. "How long, O LORD? Will you forget me forever? How long will you hide your face from me?" (13:1-2). And then on another occasion he breaks out with "Bless the LORD, O my soul, and all that is within me, bless his holy name. Bless the LORD, O my soul, and do not forget all his benefits" (103:1-2).

Even the saintly Mother Teresa, we now know, lived much of her life in what John of the Cross called "the dark night of the soul." The hills-and-valleys experience of the Christian life is graphically described in the following Parabolic Interlude found in *The Authentic Witness: Credibility and Authority*, by C. Norman Kraus.

> The rule of God is like an underground river flowing from its source high in the glaciers toward its eventual destination. Depending on the terrain, it sometimes surfaces in a quiet pool in the desert to create an oasis. Again it emerges as springs and rivulets of "still waters." And then when spring thaws melt the snow, the streams become a surging torrent, clearing old clogged channels and creating new ones for the river. Finally the great river below the ground and the surface estuaries have made their way through the rich delta country [and] merge in the ocean.
>
> Always the great river is there to be tapped by wells deep into the earth. Sometimes it gushes out under artesian pressure, and sometimes it lies cool and deep, to be reached only by disciplined human effort. But wherever it comes to the surface, it brings life and activity. People and animals flock to it for refreshment and cleansing.
>
> Just so "the river of life" flowing from the throne of God (Revelation 22:1ff.) through the terrain of human history until it emerges finally in the midst of the city of God, bringing life and healing to the nations.[2]

Our message is that serving on a faith-based board can and should be viewed as a Christian vocation. As directors work and wait their way through the everyday routine, they enter this inner sanctum of the Spirit, where they draw on the resources that God has in store for them.

Obstacles to Boards' Practicing a Deeper Spirituality

If incorporating a more conscious sense of God is so necessary, and so transformative, why is it so seldom achieved? What interferes with the good intentions of good and sincere people? What stops them from doing what their hearts know could improve their performance and increase their sense of fulfillment?

1. *Inertia.* The biggest obstacle is inertia, meaning doing things as they have always been done. It means operating out of habit rather than vision and a profound sense of corporate calling. We know the phrases: Why fix it if it isn't broken? Don't rock the boat with new ways of thinking and doing things.

A good orientation program for new directors is widely acknowledged as important. Some boards might do well to adopt a de-orientation program, jettisoning old and counterproductive ways and making room for new and better ways of doing things.

In truth, many organizations are broken; they just don't know it yet. The boardroom can be a very unsafe place for new ideas and ways of thinking. Boards that operate on little more than the momentum of past success will not be around to face the future.

2. *A false sense of well-being.* Nonprofit directors are inclined to revel in success, whether deserved or not. Their preference is to ignore problems. Management reciprocates by succumbing to the human temptation to underreport failure and overreport success, leaving a board to bask in a fool's paradise! Boards need to

A midsized faith-based nonprofit was in more trouble than the board knew. The CEO, a generous and kind-hearted individual, had served the organization for over twenty years. Under his leadership the organization had thrived and established a very good reputation nationally. However, the organization had outgrown its CEO. Financial performance was lagging. Strategic focus had become unclear. The board was increasingly anxious but reluctant to deal with the problem. In time, the board and CEO agreed to a transition. It took the courage of a few to name the problem and catalyze change.

know and then to act on what they know. Their legal and fiduciary responsibilities hold them accountable for results.

3. *Narcissism.* Many directors are, in the pointed words of Ronald Rolheiser in *The Shattered Lantern: Rediscovering a Felt Presence of God,* "unhealthily obsessed and entrapped within themselves." In short, all turned in on themselves. They feel little need for anything beyond themselves. They feel no urgency. They are satisfied to live in a state of myopic self-centeredness. They would do well to hear Robert Browning's exclamation, "Ah, but a man's reach should exceed his grasp, / Or what's a heaven for?"[3]

This narcissistic attitude, which someone has likened to an ego on steroids, is as inappropriate in the boardroom as in the personal lives of the directors. Ego is the antithesis of a service-oriented board. The Spirit cannot thrive in an atmosphere of self-sufficiency.

4. *Tyranny of time.* Time limitations are a mountain-sized obstacle to spirituality. Rolheiser refers to a question once posed to Thomas Merton about the leading spiritual disease of our time. "What Merton is pointing out here is that, regarding God and religion, our problem is not so much badness as it is busyness."

Many boards work in a hurried atmosphere, where Spirit-directed deliberation is impossible. Busy schedules often preclude attending to deeper matters. As a result, boards are inclined to neglect the very things that could move them into a higher orbit. Many boards do not use their limited meeting time wisely. They settle into a meeting routine, and members like that. But this slavish adherence to a nonproductive routine, often inherited, can also be the source of much organizational frustration and dysfunction. Instead of being open to the

CEOs learn the art of spinning. They concentrate on that part of the glass that is half full while denying the half that is empty. This eternal optimism beclouds reality and gives the appearance that things are better than they are. After several years of flagging performance, a CEO recognized that the future of the organization was in jeopardy. Instead of spin, the board began to communicate in "real talk" with the CEO and senior leadership. A process was begun that rescued the organization from oblivion.

Spirit and new ways of thinking, they continue to do what they have been doing. Some boards become locked into traditional ways of doing things and convinced that their way is the only way, when their way is actually at the heart of their problem.

The time monster can be tamed. It begins by helping directors to understand their role better as distinct from management. Boards, and especially board committees, have a tendency to arbitrarily delve into micromanagement while leaving their governance role undone or poorly done. Much board meeting time is taken up with things that are not board business. Board committees often use up more meeting time than the board itself. Simple techniques like consent agendas, the use of corporate dashboards, and well-prepared reports with actionable proposals—these can help a board use its limited time to better advantage. Board chairs and chief executives can do much to create a spirit of expectation and openness to the spiritual dimensions of their work as they prepare agendas, frame meetings, and stage agenda items.

> Books like *Doing Good Even Better* by Edgar Stoesz and the writings of John Carver on policy governance (especially *Reinventing Your Board* and *Boards That Make a Difference*) as well as material from the Independent Sector and Board Source—such works are available to help directors manage their time better while making better decisions.[4]

5. *Unclear or unrealistic expectations.* When a body is not clear in what it expects or if it expects too much too soon, the result will be confusion or discouragement or both. Enriching the soul is more like taking vitamin tablets than aspirin: the results are not immediate. Spirituality grows from within. It begins modestly and has an accumulative effect.

Pathways into the Heart and Soul for Better Service

The journey into the essence of our being, to more conscious recognition of the transcendental, is uncharted. With the apostle Paul's letter to the Corinthians, we admit that "we know only in part, and we prophesy only in part." But we look forward to the time when we "will know fully, even as [we] have been fully known" (1 Cor 13:9, 12).

A small faith-based nonprofit did not have any set time for meetings. Their occasional meetings each lasted three to four hours. Agendas were unpredictable. Attendance was uneven. Satisfaction was low. Strategic focus was lacking. In a planning session with their new executive director, the board decided to meet monthly. The agenda, it was agreed, would be drawn up by the chair and executive director. The first thirty minutes were to be devoted to worship, followed by a quick review of the executive report, followed by time to address critical issues, including fundraising. The final half hour was to be devoted to reporting, celebration, and prayer. The whole experience was transformational.

A board's constant preoccupation with *doing* must be joined by the board's *being* and *becoming*. To the apostle's counsel (2 Cor 4:18) noted at the beginning, we add one word: "Look not *only* on what can be seen." Organizations do need to take care of their daily business. What most boards find so hard to accomplish is to get beyond the daily routine and make room for the Spirit to usher them into things eternal.

Great boards in the faith tradition see themselves as servants of God, caring for God's people and participating in the care and ongoing work of creation. In short, we are stewards, not owners.

The spirituality we advocate is more than frosting on a cake. It is yeast that leavens the whole loaf. Such spirituality brings balance to life, including both the physical, which surrounds us, and the spiritual, which is God's gift to us. It waits to shine through us and illumine our actions and express itself in serving others. It brings fresh perspective to our world. It gives life meaning and purpose. It transforms us as we serve.

A new flowering of the Spirit awakens our consciousness and floods our souls with energy and enthusiasm. It liberates us from being captivated by that which will one day disappear. It helps us reach beyond ourselves. It tames our assertive egos and narcissistic tendencies and gives us a joyful heart to serve others.

In summary, a simple thought from David Young's book *Springs of Living Water* captures our hope for you and your board members. There is the *inward* look, which has us looking at ourselves and identifying our gifts and resources. There is the *outward* look, which reminds us of the needs and challenges that surround us. Finally there is the *upward* look, where we acknowledge that we are God's servants, trying earnestly to know and do God's will in a spirit of humility.[5]

The time to invite and foster this new spiritual consciousness in the boardroom is *now*. Spiritual powers are released only in the present moment. It's been said that the most important thing is to get on the path, to just get started, and the rest of the steps will come once you are on the way.

And the journey begins with *us*. We acknowledge the Spirit that is already at work within us. We do not need to wait for anyone or anything. No one can do it for us. We have only to start the journey and allow the Spirit to guide us. God is present with us always. We need to be present with God.

In the words of Isaiah 60:1, "Arise, shine; for your light has come, and the glory of the LORD has risen upon you." And be joyful!

Part 2

_____

Meditations for the Organization's Soul

5

Meditations to Celebrate Accomplishments

Introduction

Nonprofit organizations face immense challenges. Sometimes those challenges seem overwhelming. Nonprofits, however, also have much to celebrate. Almost every day executives have things to celebrate and to lament. Such is the stuff of work. Whether large or small, learning to claim and celebrate accomplishments builds confidence and capacity.

Many things are worth celebrating. Think of the possibilities: positive financial performance after years of struggle, a full personnel roster, high client satisfaction, glowing reports on a capital campaign, or completion of a major project. The list could go on!

Directors, it seems, like to picture themselves as making weighty decisions. They continually feel threatened by some calamity. Lament comes more easily than celebration.

Even routine happenings like a progress report on achieving goals, positive financial and census reports, or an encouraging report on marketing and turnover data should be viewed with appreciation. Each is a simple but powerful way that builds organizational confidence and capacity.

A senior-services provider recently did a ribbon cutting for a new facility that includes a bistro-coffee bar and some much-needed large-group activity space. The entire community was involved in the ribbon-cutting celebration. Donor appreciation events can also be an occasion for the governing board and senior leadership to express appreciation for support from multiple stakeholders. A unique celebration once occurred when two boards met to memorialize the end of the two organizations they governed and the birth of a new integrated organization with a shared mission.

Celebrating achievements is an important part of a board's strategic work. For example, the new executive director of a small nonprofit wanted to lead the board forward, in spite of some setbacks during economic turbulence. In this context, it was very important to begin the strategic work with heart-felt reflection about all the positive things that had happened during the previous two years. The conversation was real. Board members acknowledged the stresses but claimed the accomplishments. This exercise gave the board a sense of capacity to engage creatively with the new executive director in imagining fresh possibilities.

A large multisite faith-affiliated system needed to establish strategic priorities. The board took an hour to review feedback from key stakeholders and noted the quite significant accomplishments in the organization's services. The board's miniparty of celebrating its achievements was a source of positive power and momentum for the strategic work that followed.

Major achievements are seldom the result of one individual's heroic effort. Celebrating is an occasion to thank the many who have made an accomplishment possible. For faith-affiliated organizations, it's an even more important opportunity to offer profound thanks to the Creator, on whose behalf the board serves as steward.

Boards of successful ventures celebrate. Work goes better when interspersed with joyful celebration. To celebrate is to acknowledge something good. When a body pauses to acknowledge its blessings, it is just one step away from celebration. Celebration is the prelude to more good to follow. Boards that celebrate their accomplishments have more accomplishments to celebrate. The mantra that "nothing succeeds like success" is true. So count your blessings and look for excuses to celebrate. Like the children of Israel, raise an Ebenezer and declare for all to hear, "Thus far the LORD has helped us" (1 Sam 7:12).

Select a meditation from this chapter that speaks best to your situation. Feel free to inject your thoughts and adapt to your circumstance. Conclude with one of the prayers that follow, again feeling free to add to it and adapt it. Some may want to repeat the Lord's Prayer in unison or sing a song together. Use silence and thoughtful pauses. Be relaxed and worshipful. Make it your goal to set a spiritual tone that will pervade the entire meeting.

A caution for you: celebrate success, but don't let it go to your head! Many boards are distracted by a run of good news. They become overconfident. We know a company that grew quickly. It added one building after another, one product line after another. Then in an economic downturn, management made a serious miscalculation. It confidently overreached and ended up being acquired by its competitor. In retrospect, one of the partners said with new humility, "Our failure can be described in one five-letter word: P-R-I-D-E."

Celebrate Relationships

> May the God who gives endurance and encouragement
> give you the same attitude of mind toward each other that
> Christ Jesus had, so that with one mind and one voice you
> may glorify the God and Father of our Lord Jesus Christ.
> Accept one another, then, just as Christ accepted you, in
> order to bring praise to God.
> —Paul, in Romans 15:5-7 NIV

It was a hot summer day when I left the office to visit a new organization some five hours away. My purpose was to ascertain how Mennonite Central Committee should respond to a request from women in five villages hoping to be liberated from their abject poverty.

By the time I arrived, a large group of villagers were already gathered. About fifteen men sat on the floor in front of me, and about fifty women quietly sat behind them.

My presentation, based on what women in other villages were doing, was well received. When the meeting ended, the men left. The women were talking excitedly among themselves, including me in their conversation. They talked about the drudgery of their daily routines, unclean drinking water, the shortage of food, husbands who didn't have jobs and who drank too much, and daughters unable to go to school. We were pondering what they could do to change things.

Our meeting proved to be a new beginning. These oppressed women had received a vision of what was possible, even in their limited surroundings. I visited them often to encourage them and evaluate their progress. The women consistently showed evidence of understanding the causes of poverty and how to tackle it effectively.

From these village women I learned that before I am able to help someone, I must have a relationship with them. If village woman and I could not first look into each other's face and see each other as a child of God, a relationship could not take root. I had good health, nice clothes, and a good job; they had almost nothing. Yet they accepted me without reservation.

Mennonite Central Committee India partnered with this group for seven years in a friendly and productive relationship. A few years after I retired, I received a phone call from these women asking me to participate in a celebration. I tried to decline, but they insisted. The day before the celebration, they called to say that a hired driver was already en route to Calcutta to pick me up and take me to their celebration.

By midmorning the next day, I was in an open field, standing under a huge colorful *shamiana* (tent) with about five thousand other women, ready to celebrate what had been accomplished! Soon the women were telling their incredible stories to each other!

Reflecting on this experience reminds me of the importance of genuine, nonjudgmental relationships. Good does not result from service given out of an ulterior motive or for self-glorification or fame. Lives and whole villages are transformed when we simply "sow the good seed" while anticipating that in God's own time the seeds will bear fruit.

In planning and evaluating their work, directors and managers of faith-based organizations tend to concentrate on what can be quantified. Missing too often is the importance of relationships. It brings to mind the dispute Jesus had with the Pharisees as recorded in Matthew 23. After scolding them for concentrating on outward appearances and neglecting such weightier matters as justice, mercy and faith, he said, "These you should have done and not left the other undone" (cf. 23:23).

—Cynthia Peacock of Kolkata (formerly Calcutta), West Bengal, India, is director of Mennonite Central Committee India and chairs the Mennonite World Conference Deacons Commission.

Honoring the Past by Celebrating It

> For the Spirit God gave us does not make us timid, but gives
> us power, love and self-control.
> —Paul, in 2 Timothy 1:7 NIV

The Lancaster Mennonite Historical Society in Pennsylvania was looking forward to celebrating the 300th anniversary of Europeans pioneers settling in their area. Celebration is hardly a strength of these reserved, historically oriented board members. But surely, they reminded themselves, this tricentennial experience of God's leading must be observed in some appropriate way!

The board knew that God could surprise, such as when God led the children of Israel out of the wilderness. So relying on faith in God, honed over three centuries of living in what we proudly call "The Garden Spot of the World," the board took on the challenge (and risk) of creating a God-honoring celebration that the public would support.

Reticent board members stepped out of their comfort zone and began to imagine how such a program might look. They identified persons who might participate in a program that would cause this historic event to come alive for another generation. A program was drawn up, including choristers and speakers. Money was not to be overlooked: the committee found a way to finance this unbudgeted event. A congregation with a large auditorium offered to host the event.

As the date approached, the committee was anxious. They felt good about the program they had planned, but would the people come to celebrate?

They were reassured when cars began arriving an hour before the appointed beginning time. When the large auditorium was filled to capacity an hour before starting time, the overflow was directed to the basement, and then to the large vestibule. Before the program began, occupants of a long stream of cars were informed, "No more room. I'm sorry. If you find a place to park, you will not find a place in the church. We are filled to capacity."

Visionary leaders had overcome their fear and hesitation. They had sponsored an event that was waiting to happen. In one word, they had led!

That is the function of a board: to lead. It needs to read the future, to imagine what is needed, and then to lead the process that will cause it to happen. Leaders should expect God-sized surprises! Thriving institutions are led by boards that understand and perform their governance role.

The future invites boards into unfamiliar turf, without a map to guide them. Great boards overcome any spirit of timidity and boldly anticipate the future. They honor the past by celebrating it while boldly but confidently claiming God's promises of a new day awaiting.

—Ken Sensenig of Ephrata, Pennsylvania, serves as assistant director of Mennonite Central Committee East Coast and is on the board of Eastern Mennonite Missions.

God Multiplies the Gift

> He who supplies seed to the sower and bread for food will supply and multiply your seed for sowing and increase the harvest of your righteousness.
> —Paul, in 2 Corinthians 9:10

With something akin to awe, the staff and board heard the story of a single woman who had never appeared on their donor records. She had worked as a seamstress in a factory, living simply and saving much of what she earned. She willed her entire estate to the mission of the church.

Not long before she passed away, a few hundred thousand dollars that she had invested in a local telephone company became the property of a much larger company. As part of that business acquisition, her estate suddenly became worth more than two million dollars. Uncertain about the future of this new investment, her trustees cashed in the stocks, and not long afterward the large, risk-laden company went belly up.

At her death several years later, her estate proved to be the largest single gift the organization had ever received. It was quite beyond her wisdom and completely unknown to the receiving board. God had multiplied the financial fruit of a lifetime.

I marveled at the features of her story as it emerged:

- She was not wealthy. Quite to the contrary, she worked for a lifetime at one of the humblest of occupations.
- She was unknown to her benefactors. Her name had never appeared on the giving records of the organization to which she left her estate.
- She lived in seclusion from financial suitors. She had never been courted by the multitude of ministries which would have streamed to her door had they known her wealth.
- She gave with absolute generosity to a cause in which she believed. For her, there was no careful division of an estate. It all went for a single purpose.
- God multiplied her gift before it was received. No human being could take credit for some scheme of wise financial investment that created a gift of such size.

Western organizations are known for organizational finesse and focus. We hire development staff, write carefully crafted appeal letters, and monitor the health of our balance sheets. We keep accurate records, and we audit assiduously. We praise the vision and skill of those who are able to attract financial contributions to keep our programs growing and strong.

Ultimately, though, our resource base is linked to a source that lies beyond our control and our ability to predict. It lies with God.

Yes, it matters what we do. Knowledge matters. Skill makes a difference. The composition and structure of the board makes a difference. The clarity of our organizational focus and the management of our staff are important. Board policy manuals have their place. CEOs and their staff require intelligent monitoring.

But what God does matters most, as illustrated in the feeding of the five thousand. When God multiplies the gift, whether of time, talent, skill, or financial resource, we see the glory of heaven spread all around.

Like the gift of the little-known seamstress, God's multiplied gifts take us by surprise. Some are more obvious than others, but all are beautiful when given in a spirit of Christian compassion.

Today once again we celebrate the surprises of God, coming as they do in unpredictable, kaleidoscopic hues.

—Richard Showalter, Landisville, Pennsylvania, is president and CEO of Eastern Mennonite Missions, Salunga, Pennsylvania, and chairs the Mission Commission of Mennonite World Conference. He is author of *On the Way with Jesus* as well as coauthor with his wife, Jewel, of *Silk Road Pilgrimage: Discovering the Church of the East.*

Let's Have a Party

Rejoice in the Lord always: again I will say, rejoice.
—Paul, in Philippians 4:4

Accomplishments, like good news, deserve to be celebrated.

Celebration is a spiritual experience. It lifts us, however temporarily, from the seriousness and even the routine of everyday life. It is a welcome interlude that brings balance to life. All work and no celebration make Johnny and Jill dull board members. Celebration lifts the spirits and gladdens the heart. It rejuvenates the body and gives strength for the journey. It can be a lubricant that makes the world go around.

Why then do organizations celebrate so seldom? We have witnessed and been party to dozens of meetings where boards commiserated over some disappointment. But the times we have participated in anything resembling a board celebration are rare.

While writing my concluding chairman's report for American Leprosy Missions, I listed our accomplishments and concluded each with "Something to celebrate." After the third or fourth time, the obvious occurred to me: "But we never celebrated!" I was embarrassed and vowed to make up for lost time.

Upon arriving the evening before our quarterly meeting, I asked the staff to make room on the agenda for a celebration. They looked at me incredulously! Did I not realize that the agenda was full and already distributed? I replied, "I know, I know. I thought we'd cut the evening session short and then celebrate into the night." Looking into their doubtful faces, I asked, "What had you planned for our evening meal dessert?" "A cake," was the response. "Excellent. Could we keep that for the celebration? Are there some candles around?"

Diane volunteered, "A closet full, held over from a fundraiser." She volunteered to get some balloons and streamers. Chris offered a favorite celebratory CD. On short notice I asked Carol to emcee the event.

We recessed the evening session a little early. The directors descended the stairs apprehensively. Quickly the mood was transformed by the sound of lively music. Balloons and streamers came into view. For a few moments we stood silently and a little awkwardly. Then Carol picked up with a few appropriate remarks, followed by more awkward silence. Clearly we did not know how to celebrate.

Feeling some responsibility to dispel the anxiety, I stepped forward hesitatingly. I selected a candle from the table. Nervously I lit it and, facing the group, I held it high and said, "Here is to the memory of Mike, who served us faithfully as treasurer and whose friendship we all miss."

The ice had been broken. One after another, the directors and senior staff came forward to light a candle and offer a celebratory comment. We forgot about time as everyone joined in the celebration. At the end of the evening, our table of lit candles looked like an altar, causing some to ask where the fire extinguisher was located. Around the edges directors were heard to say, "We must do this again soon."

Some organizations, admittedly, have more to celebrate than others, but all have something to celebrate, and all boards will have more to celebrate if they celebrate what there is. Celebration is a time to recognize and mark progress. It is an antidote for discouragement. It is the launching pad for new initiatives. Creativity thrives in a celebratory atmosphere.

Celebration and gratitude are closely related, and gratitude is an important part of spirituality. People and organizations that are spiritually strong and healthy pause to celebrate when good things happen.

—Edgar Stoesz of Akron, Pennsylvania, is retired from Mennonite Central Committee. He has served on many nonprofit boards, including chair of Habitat for Humanity International and Heifer International. He is author of numerous books, including *Doing Good Even Better*.

Rejoice and Celebrate the Ordinary

> Rejoice in the Lord always; again I will say, Rejoice. Let your gentleness be known to everyone. The Lord is near. Do not worry about anything, but in everything by prayer and supplication with thanksgiving let your requests be made known to God. And the peace of God, which surpasses all understanding, will guard your hearts and your minds in Christ Jesus.
>
> —Paul, in Philippians 4:4-7

Celebrating and rejoicing in life's ordinary gifts can enable us to recognize the many opportunities before us. The attitude of celebration helps unleash our energy and creativity to embrace and promote the vision and mission of our organization. As a board, we can talk about the many strengths and virtues of our organization, but living in an attitude of celebration is different. Our extravagant God invites us to live in a spirit of rejoicing and celebration.

Attitudes in our society often push us to espouse a worldview based on fear, scarcity, and competition. If we choose to believe it, this fear becomes a self-fulfilling prophecy. But our God is a God of abundance. God gave us an abundant world, and it is our choice to embrace a grateful outlook or to succumb to fear. Board members frequently set the organizational tone for an institution. We must learn to highlight positive trends, to work with obstacles, and to continue striving toward the goals of our organization. We are reflectors of our institution. Much as a dour outlook breeds apprehension, so a positive Inner Light brightens the vision of those around us. Let's celebrate what is already working well!

Although it may appear to be paradoxical, celebrating what is right about our organization also helps us to harness the energy we need to fix what's wrong. Rejoicing in the many ordinary things that are right will help us to be more prepared to address the issues that need attention. When we recognize the good, we're implicitly acknowledging that solutions do exist for the challenges that lay before us.

Approaching budget cuts in a challenging economy and addressing staff issues are not easy. In Paul's letter to the Philippians, his invitation to "rejoice" flies in the face of the world's pervasive attitude of scarcity. Looking on the bright side may sound naive to the cynics of the world. But we are invited to "let [our] requests be made known to God. And the peace of God, which surpasses all understanding, will guard [our] hearts and [our] minds in Christ Jesus." We are in the world but not of the world, and our abundant God is not fearful.

Making a conscious effort to celebrate and rejoice in ordinary events that are going well can help all of us become more effective in fulfilling the vision and mission of our organization. We can nurture our grateful attitudes so that our commitments to our tasks become more creative and rewarding.

"Never doubt that a small group of thoughtful, committed people can change the world," said Margaret Meade. "Indeed, it is the only thing that ever has." Again, I say, rejoice! Let's celebrate the many gifts of our organization, both ordinary and extraordinary, and by God's grace we will have the energy and creativity to address the challenges we face.

—Sharon and Anne Waltner live in Freeman, South Dakota. Sharon served as moderator of Mennonite Church USA in 2007–9 and is a healthcare facilities leadership consultant. Daughter Anne completed a doctorate of musical arts degree and contemplates farming as a vocation.

Kingdom Moments

> Our Father in heaven, . . . Your kingdom come.
> Your will be done, on earth as it is in heaven.
> —Jesus, in Matthew 6:9-10

I call them "Kingdom Moments," those brief experiences after which one says from deep within the quiet soul, "That is what the kingdom of God is all about."

Esparza, Costa Rica: eleven of us arrived at the little hotel, changed into work clothes, picked up our tools, and walked to Maria's house. Maria was a woman of forty years, short in height and slight of stature. Her smile was quick and she seemed to be energized, knowing that her old house was about to be replaced with a new one.

One look at her old house energized us all, and we tore into our work with the vigor one would use to fight a destructive fire. A spirit invaded the group, now enlarged by the presence of several of Maria's friends and neighbors. We ripped that old shack apart with hammers and hands. Roof and rafters came down first, then the simple and termite-eaten walls. There were no windows and only a simple door with no lock. Spiders, ants, termites, scorpions, roaches, and centipedes all fled in fright as their home of many years tumbled down around them. An ancient kitchen cabinet was saved for the new house. The dirt floor, packed down by the bare feet of so many years, now stood naked, baking in the first sunlight that had fallen upon it for decades.

Boards from the old house were piled near the rickety outhouse, to be split and used as firewood for cooking beans and rice. "Good riddance," we thought. Humans, created in God's image, should not live in such squalor. Animals perhaps, but not persons such Maria.

We joined hands in a circle—Maria's hands, her neighbors' hands, and our hands. We had a prayer, saying goodbye to an old house that had died. We thanked God for its years of service and spoke of the resurrection of the new house, bringing dignity, comfort, security, and safety to Maria and her family. It was a Kingdom Moment. Several hundred blocks came and were stacked at the end of a long path. The word rippled through the community, "Come and carry blocks." The procession began. Maria led the way with a glowing smile that said, "It is really happening." A little girl of perhaps six years, but four years in size, ran each trip to pick up her next block. A strong young man proudly carried five each trip, while most of us settled for two.

The blocks were moved by a procession of God's children, young and old, rich and poor, educated and illiterate. Each lugged what they could carry, and no one grumbled that another was slacking. The smile and nods that were exchanged along the path affirmed that this was indeed a Kingdom Moment.

And so it was: long bucket brigades moved tons of wet cement. Hands joined hands to move lumber. The entire community turned out to dig the foundation ditch, with even small children pitching in.

At noon of the last day, we gathered at Maria's house, now complete, for a quiet celebration. Our prayer circle joined the hands of Maria and her family, of Omar the chief carpenter, of neighbors and friends, and of the eleven Global Village volunteers. Small gifts were exchanged, and Maria received a handmade wooden plaque for the wall of her new home. It was a Kingdom Moment.

Recount and reflect on the Kingdom Moments in your organization. Thank God for them in the presence of each other, and take some time to be truly thankful.

—Mel West of Columbia, Missouri, is a retired United Methodist pastor and board service veteran for nonprofits such as Heifer International and Habitat for Humanity International. He is founder of PET (Personal Energy Transportation) Project, providing hand-cranked wheelchairs to leg-handicapped persons worldwide.

Ebenezer: Thus Far the Lord Has Helped Us

Then Samuel took a stone and set it up between Mizpah
  and Jeshanah
and named it Ebenezer [Stone of Help]; for he said,
"Thus far the LORD has helped us."

—1 Samuel 7:12

Once a year, the board of directors of Bridge of Hope National builds an Ebenezer altar. When we gather each April for our national board retreat, we celebrate the close of one fiscal year and the beginning of another. We begin by retelling the story from 1 Samuel 7, where Samuel took a stone and named it "Ebenezer," saying, "thus far the LORD has helped us." Then we take small stones and one by one lay them on a table around a lit candle as we take turns naming aloud the specific ways that we have seen God's leading us or sensed God at work within our midst.

This powerful tradition has overflowed into our annual Bridge of Hope affiliate conference, where affiliate board and staff also build an Ebenezer altar at the end of our three days together. It is our way of naming how we are seeing God at work, through both the ordinary and the extraordinary events of the past year.

This worshipful naming of God's leading among us becomes a powerful reminder, both in times of excitement and in times of discouragement, that God has led us in the past and will again lead us in the months and years ahead. Just as God faithfully led the children of Israel during the time of Samuel and beyond, so too will God show us the way as leaders of Christian faith-based organizations.

Where is the place that faith lives and moves in your organization? If you cannot locate God's movement in your board and staff, then donors and supporting churches are unlikely to see God in your midst either. And if they don't see God in your midst, they are denying themselves the boundless resources that God offers freely to all who call on God's name. There will be little reason for them to join your mission!

Even on days when we as leaders cannot find the hope or inspiration to locate faith anywhere within ourselves or our organization—and those days and months will come—we can remember our history and recognize that God was in our midst. And in the telling and reviewing of our own God story, we may find our spirits renewed and refreshed.

Set a stone in the middle of the table where you are holding your board meeting. Take time at your next meeting to go around your board table, asking each person to name one way they have seen God at work in this past year. Pause and express gratitude to God for these concrete evidences of God's help and leading. "Ebenezer, thus far the LORD has helped us."

—Edith Yoder of Exton, Pennsylvania, serves as executive director of Bridge of Hope National, a Christian faith-based nonprofit whose vision is to end and prevent homelessness for women and children across the United States by calling churches into action.

Prayers

*At the end of each chapter, we offer three prayers for concluding
a meditation. Select the one that seems most suitable to your setting, and feel free to amend or supplement as seems best in your
circumstance. Some may also invite all in attendance to pray the
Lord's Prayer in unison.*

God of all creation,
   God of all time,
      God of all that was, is, and will be
  We begin this meeting by acknowledging your presence in our midst.
    Clear our minds and open our hearts to be receptive to your spirit.
[*Pause.*]

We thank you for the beauty of your creation. With the psalmist
  we say,
   "When [we] look at your heavens, the work of your fingers,
      the moon and the stars that you have established;
   what are human beings that you are mindful of them?"
     [Ps 8:3-4]

Who are we that you should pay any attention to us?
  Yet you shower us with an everlasting love,
    and for that we give you our thanks.
[*Pause.*]

Today we thank you in a special way for hearing our prayer in
behalf of [*name the good news being celebrated and elaborate
as useful*]. Truly we say, every good and perfect gift comes from,
you, the giver of all good. We receive your gift with gratitude and
acknowledge the responsibility it places on us to use it wisely.
[*Pause.*]

Thank you for permitting us this small part in the work of your
great kingdom. Make us, we pray, worthy servants.
  Give us a heart of compassion.
  Give us wisdom to see the future clearly.

Grant us a spirit of humility.
Grant us joy in your service.
For it is in your name that we render this service and offer this prayer of thanks.

And all the people said Amen.
Amen and Amen.

—Edgar Stoesz of Akron, Pennsylvania, has worked for Mennonite Central Committee and served on many nonprofit boards, including chairing Habitat for Humanity International. He is author of numerous books, including *Doing Good Even Better*.

We gather in prayer. Remembering the past—the vision, the dreams, the struggles, the work, the leaders, and all who have contributed to our present reality.

Thanks be to God.

We gather in prayer. Celebrating the present—the goals accomplished, the projects completed, the objectives reached, the barriers crossed, the board's success.

Thanks be to God.

We gather in prayer. Anticipating the future—the yet-to-be developed projects, the personnel waiting to serve, the communities hoping for change, the possibilities of [*name of the organization, church, nonprofit*] to accomplish good.

Thanks be to God.
Amen.

—Dorothy Nickel Friesen has spent her professional career in the English classroom as a teacher and the last twenty-eight years as a Mennonite pastor, seminary administrator, and conference minister.

∞

Happily, O Lord, and humbly we rejoice in doing what we do and doing it well, in planning and following through, in working hard and seeing results. We dedicate our success to you, knowing that you are the author of all that is good and perfect. Amen.

—David Johnson Rowe is copastor of Greenfield Hill Congregational Church, Fairfield, Connecticut.

6

Meditations When Faced with Major Disappointments

Introduction

It's a rare board and executive that has not encountered significant setbacks. The illustrations abound: a capable CFO resigns, a major contract is canceled, or a major donor is lost. The organization may find itself mired in a serious recession or faced with the disappointing consequences of a strategic decision. Although most organizations are familiar with disappointments or big set-

71

backs, many are loath to acknowledge them or, more significantly, to learn from them.

Many organizations struggle with projects that never materialize. Economic turbulence has forced many nonprofits to abandon major new projects. Boards have to deal with strategic priorities that cannot be achieved because of severe resource constraints. An organization we are familiar with needed to explain to major donors why a large capital campaign had to be significantly downsized because the second phase of the campaign had fallen short. These disappointments can be extremely difficult to weather.

> A college board and executive staff, indeed, the entire organization, had to deal with negative feedback from an external stakeholder objecting to a decision made by the executive staff and released in the public. In retrospect, the board regretted that it had not engaged more thoughtfully in the process, although the resulting decisions might not have been different. It was important that the board acknowledges its role in the dilemma.

In other cases, key leaders don't deliver on promises or have lapses in moral or ethical judgments. Occasionally governing boards need to terminate an executive who has violated professional boundaries in relationship(s). These can be extremely demanding and demoralizing circumstances.

To face disappointment and setbacks, great boards draw on spiritual resources and experience. Crises and setbacks are also opportunities. When a key staff member or officer resigns, instead of freezing in fear, directors should look on it as an opportunity to identify new leadership within the organization, or to draw new skills into their ranks. Crisis makes it easier to effect change. It helps leaders to realign priorities for responding to changing demands.

Processing a disappointment begins by facing facts for what they are and adopting a course of action that will help them survive and ultimately prosper. Jim Collins calls this "real talk," in which nothing is whitewashed or varnished.

Second, the board, working with management, looks for opportunity beyond the crisis. The great industrialist Andrew Carnegie discovered that a recession was the best time to tool up for the boom period that was sure to follow. An effective board asks, "What can we learn from this?" There is wisdom in the dictum "Don't waste a good crisis!"

Finally, faith-affiliated organizations balance accountability with grace. Disappointments are an opportunity to demonstrate that the spiritual dimension of our work makes a real difference. We are familiar with an organization that was taking a real beating from external sources. In the process the board acknowledged that it had failed to engage appropriately in the decision-making process. The board needed wisdom and courage to strike a balance between supporting the executive while also processing strong negative feedback from key external stakeholders. The potential for the board and CEO relationship to rupture was great. Grace and trust prevented that from occurring.

Without venture, little is gained. Hence, good boards will continue to venture, and the odds are good to realize mistakes and disappointments along the way.

Select a meditation from this chapter that speaks best to a situation facing you. Insert your thoughts and adapt to your circumstance. Feel free to explore the meditations from other chapters. Conclude with one of the prayers that follow, feeling free to add and adapt. Some may want to repeat the Lord's Prayer in unison or sing a song together. Use silence and thoughtful pauses. Be relaxed and worshipful. Make it your goal to set a spiritual tone that will pervade the entire meeting.

Failure Need Not Be Fatal

> But Peter said, "Man, I do not know what you are talking
> about!" At that moment, while he was still speaking, the
> cock crowed. The Lord turned and looked at Peter. Then
> Peter remembered the word of the Lord, how he had said
> to him, "Before the cock crows today, you will deny me
> three times." And he went out and wept bitterly.
>
> —Luke 22:60-62

We laid out a plan to return to profitability. The plan had nine straightforward steps, each assigned to a management person for action. Our hope was to save the company from closing down.

The CEO set the plan into action: overtime and salaries were cut, some employees were laid off, inventories were reduced, product pricing was refined, supplier relationships were renegotiated, and these actions were all communicated to everyone involved. After a number of sleepless nights, our plan was implemented and the future looked more hopeful.

A review of our results presented to the next board meeting looked promising; the numbers were moving in the right direction, and employees were adjusting to a new reality. The crisis appeared to be over. Management was spending its time on positive activities instead of fighting fires and fending off a nervous bank.

Yet within just two months the market for building supplies began to shrink even further. Housing starts were down to pre-1950 levels, and foreclosures were on the rise. Our market was collapsing around us. There was no way out: we had to sell or close. We had failed.

My first reaction was to look for something or someone to blame. After all, who could have predicted that things would become so bad? We had thought that our plan was the ticket to continued solvency. Even the bank agreed that our strategy was on target. Yet—I had to admit, the rest of the board had to admit, and our CEO had to admit—we had failed.

This experience taught me that what appears to be failure can actually be seen as paying tuition for a learning experience.

What we were so sure was right turned out to be wrong, and the result was failure.

The apostle Peter failed. His spirit must have been in the dregs when, after denying Jesus for the third time, his eyes met Jesus' eyes, and Scripture tells us that he wept bitterly. He had failed miserably. But then Peter regained his footing. He was forgiven for his failure and rose to play a critical role in building the church. I have a hunch that Peter's bitter failure matured him in ways that nothing else could have done. Failure may actually have been a necessary part of Peter's later success as a leader.

When your organization, whether for profit or nonprofit, is on the edge—income is down, needs and costs are increasing, leadership is discouraged, and directors question the future—then remember Peter. Be reminded that failure need not be fatal. God's light shines brightest in the darkness of our deepest despair.

> As the evening twilight fades away,
> The sky is filled with stars, invisible by day.
> —Henry Wadsworth Longfellow,
> in "Morituri Salutamus"

—R. Lee Delp of Lansdale, Pennsylvania, is a boardroom veteran of both for profit and nonprofit organizations.

Ora et Labora, **Pray and Work**

> Think for a moment about the birds of the sky. They don't
> plant. They don't harvest. They don't store up in barns. Even
> so, your spiritual Father cares for them. Really now, aren't
> you all more precious than birds? Besides, who of you, by
> fretting and fuming, can make yourself one inch taller?
> —Jesus, in Matthew 6:26-27, Cotton Patch Version

To practice a life of prayer, Abba Antony went to live in the desert, but all sorts of thoughts distracted him. "Lord, I want to be saved," he cried, "but these thoughts do not leave me alone. What shall I do in my affliction? How can I be saved?" Outside his cell, Antony saw a monk making rope, then getting up to pray, then sitting down again to work, then getting up to pray again. When Antony heard the Lord speak to him, he understood that the monk he had been watching was an angel, sent in answer to his prayer. "Do this and you will be saved," the angel said to Antony.

At Koinonia Farm we work at our equivalent of "making rope," but we intentionally set aside time for prayer throughout the day, too. This rhythm has taken deep root here. Prayer and work sustains us.

It is a Friday afternoon in April, the last day of our board meeting. Springtime is cool in the air. Land and animals are fully awake from winter slumber. It's been a good meeting, with time built in for both prayer and work. But we're humans, and all too soon our thoughts of God and creation fade; we become the center of our world and take ourselves far too seriously.

Optimism gives way to furrowed brows as we discuss how to replace a community home destroyed by fire. It seems ironic that the place, so instrumental to the partnership-housing move-ment—Koinonia gave birth to both Habitat for Humanity and the Fuller Center for Housing—would struggle so mightily to replace a much-needed house. How will we find the capital to take care of our aging facilities, never mind build a new house?

Then a board member shares the story of an Oxford-educated fellow who came to help an intentional Christian community much like ours that was having difficulties. He asked, "How many times are we instructed in Scripture to love God, and how many times are we instructed to love our neighbor?" He answered his own question: "Well, I went through the whole book with a highlighter and found that the number of verses about loving our neighbor wins two to one."

The story sends us into a prayerful silence. As we hear the sounds of nature drifting through the open windows, we are reminded once more that God is at the center of the world: we are not the center. When we return to our work, in walks the beginning executive director of New Horizons, the local Habitat Affiliate. A tall exuberant man, he apologizes for interrupting our meeting, but he is in the area and can't wait to share the news that New Horizons and the Fuller Center for Housing are ready to partner in rebuilding the house destroyed by fire. He hopes we will accept.

I look across the table at a fellow board member. His eyes are open wide in surprise. I mouth to him the word "Amen." He smiles. Big.

Many of us feel personally responsible for the organizations we help lead. Isn't a board of directors expected to be in charge? Don't we have every right to fret and fume? After all, isn't it the board that saves the organization? We can easily get caught in this rut. That's when God gently reminds us that we are not God: we are God's instruments. We make rope; we pray. "Do this and you will be saved," the angel said to Antony.

—Bren Dubay of Americus, Georgia, is executive director of Koinonia Farm, an intentional Christian community founded by Clarence and Florence Jordan and Mabel and Martin England.

Where Is God in All of This?

I will sing of your steadfast love, O LORD, forever;
with my mouth I will proclaim your faithfulness to all generations.
I declare that your steadfast love is established forever;
your faithfulness is as firm as the heavens.
—Psalm 89:1-2

With those words, the chair of the Fresno Pacific University board reconvened the trustees for the second day of the regular fall meeting. The bottom was dropping out of the economy, and the nation was slipping into what we now call the Great Recession. Fall enrollments had come in significantly below expectations. As a result, the university had to reduce spending and plan for an uncertain future. No one knew how bad the economic meltdown would ultimately become. The board directed the university administration to cut costs, to evaluate (and possibly terminate) programs that were not cost-effective, and to propose new initiatives for increasing revenue. University leaders were told to develop a worst-case scenario.

Against that backdrop, the board chair directed our attention to Psalm 89. God had promised King David that his descendants would rule Israel forever, but now the king has suffered defeat in a battle, is scorned by neighbors, and feels forsaken by God, who has let enemies ruin some of the king's strongholds. Order has given way to chaos.

Many in Israel are asking, "Where is God in all of this?" The psalmist Ethan the Ezrahite, a contemporary of Solomon, responds by affirming God's faithfulness in spite of enormous upheaval. Israel prays for God to keep his promise to David, restore their earthly leader, and bring relief to a nation caught in a social and political crisis. Yet even amid this uncertainty and change, the psalmist declares God's steadfast love and faithfulness (v. 2). As Christians, we are reminded of fulfillment in a different way than expected: the promised Messiah—Jesus—would come through the line of David, bringing hope to all.

In times of crisis, nonprofit boards can be overwhelmed. Faith-based organizations are not exempt from distress. Problem-solving sessions can spiral downward into self-defeating discussions that undermine confidence and limit the ability to plan creatively for the future. Shocked by circumstances, but forced to make difficult decisions with inadequate information, some boards wring their hands and become paralyzed.

Other boards grow stronger during times of crisis because of members' shared faith in God, deep commitment to the organization's mission, and high level of trust in each other. Effective boards acknowledge the facts, however difficult. Knowing that their trust lies in God, the ultimate source of knowledge, these boards move on to analyze the problems before them and collectively search for effective solutions.

Several factors can help boards move forward during times of crisis. First, remember that we not only serve a faithful God, but we also do his work. God's presence provides confidence in the present and offers hope for the future. Second, a clear affirmation of the mission can renew the trustees' sense of call, which got them involved in the organization in the first place.

When boards look to God and remember their mission, it's much easier to take on difficult and complex challenges. As members combine their knowledge and experience, they gain new insights as a group. Disparate ideas become new solutions that go beyond what any individual could imagine. Not only does this result in better solutions to difficult problems; it also builds trust within the board and confidence in their own decisions.

We do the work of God. In times of crisis, it's important for boards to remember that God is faithful, and as the psalmist says, his steadfast love is established forever.

—D. Merrill Ewert of Fresno, California, is president of Fresno Pacific University.

Risking a Disappointment on God

> We also glory in our sufferings, because we know that
> suffering produces perseverance; perseverance, character;
> and character, hope. And hope does not put us to shame,
> because God's love has been poured out into our hearts
> through the Holy Spirit, who has been given to us.
> —Paul, in Romans 5:3-5 NIV

I have learned that people are human and that life is not always fair, in my way of thinking! In every organization there are politics that influence decisions; there are outside laws and regulations that one cannot always control; others can have different views and philosophies; people are human and let us down sometimes—all of which can result in disappointment. I have experienced many levels of disappointment, ranging from little disappointments to devastating disappointments, such as someone whom I respected and trusted letting me down with unscrupulous behavior.

My reaction to disappointment is often anger and focused on the unfairness of the situation. It is easy to stay within my box and not look outside of myself or the immediate situation. Yes, I persevere through it, but I fail to intentionally use the disappointment to strengthen myself or expand my horizons, even though it usually has that effect.

Today I view many of the disappointments that I have experienced as having played vital learning lessons in my life, despite their painfulness at the time. In looking back, disappointments have led me down a more-productive or different path. Disappointments have forced me to broaden my vision; they have helped me to be smarter in the way I do or say things. Disappointments have even helped me to experience a deeper or different understanding of life, another person, or even myself!

My "ah-ha" moment was when I finally realized that God sees the big picture while I have tunnel vision. I accepted the reminder that God makes "all things work together for good" (Rom 8:28). God truly is in control of the situation! If I would just step aside and recognize that fact, disappointment might be replaced with hope and a different vision.

I am still working on accepting my reactions to disappointment and on leaning on the Lord for guidance through the disappointment. "Let go, let God" is the mantra I aspire to in these situations. True faith is risking the situation on God, allowing God to open my mind to learning and providing opportunities for hope.

Our challenge is to learn from disappointment, to look for how God will navigate us through this situation. Let's risk the situation on God. God can handle it!

—Kendall Hunsicker of Lititz, Pennsylvania, is vice president of healthcare services at Willow Valley Retirement Communities, Lancaster, Pennsylvania.

Responding to Life's Disappointments

The God of heaven will give us success. We his servants
will start rebuilding.
—Nehemiah, in Nehemiah 2:20 NIV

Rarely does life go as we hope and expect. Disappointment and discouragement are often unavoidable realities in both our personal lives as well as in our public involvements. New ventures start up: some succeed and some fail. So how do we react and what can be learned when our lives and our ventures take unexpected turns for the worst?

The Scriptures recount the challenges faced by God's people over the centuries. Some of life's tragedies are the result of personal or communal failings. Others are due to conditions beyond human control. We can learn much from the experiences of Nehemiah and the courageous group of returning exiles.

Biblical scholars consider the destruction of Jerusalem and the exile to Babylon of 586 BC as a major event, second only to the great exodus out of Egypt for impacting the nation of Israel. A new normal had been established. Nehemiah made his return to Jerusalem some decades after the fall of the city known as Zion. He sets the tone for the rest of the book when he says courageously: "We his servants will start rebuilding." And so they did. And so can we.

Those years in Babylonian exile brought about many changes for the people of Israel. One of those changes was the establishment of the first synagogue. Synagogues were not intended to replace the temple; rather, they were meant to be places of prayer in the absence of the temple.

In addition, with the Israelite return came a spiritual renewal, including increased interest in reading and studying Torah, the Hebrew Scriptures. The new normal meant a return to the worship of God and rebuilding of community. The reign of kings also ended with the exile. People no longer had the mediating and sometimes meddling presence of an earthly king to get in the way of their allegiance and loyalty to God.

All these changes took place as Nehemiah was rebuilding the walls surrounding the city of Jerusalem. Nehemiah gathered these returning exiles and gave them a sense of purpose and a reason to be hopeful. Brick by brick they rebuilt their city, their religious practices, and their sense of community.

- What needs rebuilding in your organization?
- What are the technical and adaptive changes necessary to move ahead?
- We usually think about walls being torn down. What are the walls and structures that may need rebuilding and repair?
- What kind of spiritual renewal may be needed in our lives as leaders when we experience disappointment and discouragement?

Is God still able to restore a people and renew a vision? History suggests that this restoration is exactly what our God does best. One brick at a time, God is able to rebuild and restore his people and their passion. But it will require courage to let go of the past and allow a new vision and work of the spirit to blow as it will.

> Therefore, if anyone is in Christ, there is a new creation: every-thing old has passed away; see, everything has become new!
> —Paul, in 2 Corinthians 5:17

—Beryl Jantzi of Harrisonburg, Virginia, is a pastor and directs stewardship education for Everence, a financial and mutual aid organization.

Overcoming Disappointment

> And not only that, but we also boast in our sufferings, knowing that suffering produces endurance, and endurance produces character, and character produces hope, and hope does not disappoint us, because God's love has been poured into our hearts through the Holy Spirit that has been given to us.
>
> —Paul, in Romans 5:3-6

Few disappointments are more painful than experiencing the death of a child. Feeling this loss is as dark, helpless, and alone as possible. It comes with a sense of betrayal and unfairness that strike our very core and challenge our belief systems. It might be human nature to search for learning in these times of grief that threaten despair. Parenthood is not always joyful and fulfilling. It can involve many levels of disappointment. These disappointments result in lots of learning, preparing us for other responsibilities.

Organizational leadership can seem a lot like ownership or power and authority. Our deep commitment can cause us to take things personally and react very strongly. As in parenthood, organizational leadership includes times of deep disappointment. Although sometimes expected, these disappointments are still discouraging. They can feel devastating. We find ourselves asking, "Now what?" We have to try again, or do something different. If we have the patience to persevere, things usually turn out better than hoped for when we find a different approach.

Finding this new approach may require us to acknowledge that we don't know everything and that we don't get to control or decide all things. It can be humbling and certainly frustrating. However, disappointments are also an opportunity to step back, reevaluate and clarify our focus, and choose healthy individual and organizational processes. We should probably even be asking ourselves some questions: What did we miss? What *really* is our goal or purpose?

Jeremiah 29:11-14 can speak to us: "'For I know the plans I have for you,' declares the LORD, 'plans to prosper you and not to harm you, plans to give you hope and a future. Then you will call on me and come and pray to me, and I will listen to you. You will seek me and find me when you seek me with all your heart. I will be found by you,' declares the LORD" (NIV).

It is valuable for boards to reflect when things don't go well. Shared perspectives and encouragement can provide healing and deepen a sense of purpose and resolve to move forward. The board can express solidarity with executive leadership and acknowledge its own role and responsibility for the difficulty encountered.

As we work through a disappointment, it is comforting and constructive for us to draw on our faith and feel confident that all will be well. "Many are the plans in a person's heart," says Proverbs 19:21, "but it is the LORD's purpose that prevails" (NIV).

As in all situations, it is important to keep things in proper perspective and maintain a positive outlook. This is especially true for those in leadership, since others look to them to inspire hope.

—Jessie Kaye is president and chief executive officer of Prairie View, a mental health agency in Newton, Kansas.

God Is Amazing

When two Mennonite churches merged, the new denomination inherited a number of buildings in Newton, Kansas. They were all storefront buildings that previously housed the national offices for the General Conference Mennonite Church.

With the formation of a new church, fewer staff were needed in the Newton offices. As the denomination went through the normal growing pains of any new organization, staffing changes and adjustments continued.

New technologies allowed people to work all across the country. A new phone system allowed receptionists to work from anywhere, thus there was no longer a need for receptionists. These changes had direct impact on the number of staff in the Newton office.

As the number of staff in Newton began to decrease, the staffs in several locations began praying for a solution. The Newton building was listed with a real estate agent. We were open to selling or renting office space.

We received an offer to purchase one of the buildings. The offer was low and our counteroffer wasn't accepted. The potential buyer also ran into other problems. We were disappointed.

Another Mennonite organization expressed some interest, but some physical changes were needed to making the space work for them. We were attracted to sharing our space with them; but in the end we both agreed that it was not a suitable location for them. Emotionally, it was not easy to give up this possibility.

Then a group inquired about renting some of our space. They were a social-service organization and provided an important ministry in the community. Their mission and activities would have been quite compatible with the staff in the Newton offices. We thought it was an answer to prayer.

All of this was taking place during the recession. Consequently, rental space was abundant in Newton, and many buildings were for sale. The potential buyer decided on another building. We were very disappointed.

Months later, a new potential buyer appeared, made an offer, and also expressed interest in some of our additional buildings. We agreed on a price and sold the properties.

For staff who had been praying, it was a spiritual experience. The offer and the possibility of selling additional buildings was beyond what anyone had expected. Some described it as a holy moment. After experiencing so many disappointments along the way, this was the answer to prayer. And the sale price was much better than any of the previous offers. God provided more than we had hoped or dreamed of.

Taking our organizational concerns to God is not something we'll find in a business textbook. Yet if we allow God to be part of our decision making, it is amazing what God will do. Waiting on God may not be recognized as sound business, but it is the wise thing for a Christian organization to do.

> Thank you, God, for your faithfulness.
> Thank you that you care for us, that you care for the
>   work we do.
> Give us the wisdom to wait when decisions and directions
>   are not obvious.
> Help us to wait upon you, O God.
> In the name of your Son. Amen.

—Marty Lehman of Elkhart, Indiana, is associate executive director for churchwide operations for Mennonite Church USA.

Overheated Relationships

> To be grateful for the good things that happen in our lives is easy, but to be grateful for all our lives—the good as well as the bad, the moments of joy as well as the moments of sorrow, the successes as well as the failures, the rewards as well as the rejections—that requires hard spiritual work. Still, we are only truly grateful people when we can say "thank you" to all that has brought us to the present moment. . . . Let's not be afraid to look at everything that has brought us to where we are now and trust that we will soon see in it the guiding hand of a loving God.
>
> —Henri Nouwen[1]

A single significant difficult event can trigger a ripple effect through out the organization that can be discouraging or even disastrous to the staff, board, and even the clients. The event can be as simple as the resignation of a beloved employee, a rejection of a long-sought important grant or donation, or a major financial setback. The event can be complex, like the embezzlement of funds by a trusted staff member, the betrayal of confidence by a long-term board member, or a criminal allegation. Discouraging events can have a cumulative negative effect on everyone.

Over the long warm spring, the staff became very aware that the air-conditioning system was not doing well. The board's greatest fear was realized when it learned that the system was too old to fix. The cost for replacement exceeded the available resources. After donors refused to provide what was needed, a grant was sought. When the first rejection letter came, the staff continued to keep high hopes even while the temperature also rose as the summer progressed. By the time the second grant was rejected, it was becoming difficult for staff to work in the extreme heat. They wondered if the board cared about their well-being. Board members felt helpless and unable to fix the problem. The administrative staff blamed themselves for the grant rejections.

Eventually a solution emerged through creative thinking and teamwork. Funding was identified for the work in smaller stages, and emergency work was initiated.

The task that remained was repairing relationships between staff, administration, and board. Meetings with board members gave staff a time to vent their frustration and gave board members a time to express appreciation for their suffering in uncomfortable working conditions.

Surprisingly long after the solution was found, the staff, board, and clients found that relationships had not only been restored but had also been strengthened. Though no one wants a crisis, the opportunity to care for each other while solving problems created new opportunities.

It is easy to thank God when something wonderful happens. It is almost impossible to thank God for the moments when all seems lost. Yet every experience that we have personally and corporately becomes part of the makeup of who were are. Every rejection becomes an opportunity to find a new creative response. The journey of life moves us from one place to another with an often-invisible guiding hand that leads us, if only we trust in God's plan. In all of that, we rejoice and praise the Creator.

—Kathryn Goering Reid of Waco, Texas, is executive director of Family Abuse Center. She earlier served as an administrator for the Church of the Brethren and as a pastor of Austin Mennonite Church.

Seeing with the Heart

> Now to him who by the power at work within us is able
> to accomplish abundantly far more than all we can ask or
> imagine, to him be glory in the church and in Christ Jesus
> to all generations, forever and ever. Amen.
> —Paul, in Ephesians 3:20-21

> We are dealing with God's mix, people made in God's image,
> a compelling mystery.
> —Max De Pree[2]

I have observed that leaders in my church tend to spiritualize things too much. This raises the ante higher than it was meant to be. In matters of Christian faith, we often forget about our humanity. If we would confess our humanity, perhaps we could begin to deal with being made in God's image—a compelling mystery that is present in each board meeting, particularly when faced with enormous questions of direction and destiny.

The agenda of a large meeting of general boards was designed to evaluate the progress of merging three church bodies. The progress had been uncertain at best.

I should have read the signs at the onset of meeting: delays in members' arrival by a March snowstorm, being seated on a stage that was inadequate for our numbers. Those by the edge of the stage seemed only one chair's scoot from crashing five feet to the auditorium floor.

These were signs of precarious positions that board members brought with them, ending up in a stormy debate. Some came convinced of the position they had arrived at while others were seemingly perplexed, even confused. Was this to be a meeting with only winners and losers emerging from the fray?

Then the meeting moderator, acting from exasperation as much as from certainty and wisdom, divided the meeting into two national factions: the United States and Canada. I don't know what the Canadians did, but we U.S. folk removed our chairs from behind the tables and formed a circle at midstage. Symbolically leaving our dockets and agenda behind, we spoke to each other from our hearts, revealing our humanness. The tone was somber but increasingly hopeful as board members one by one opened the curtains that hid their positions and perspectives for all to view in raw reality. Confession of hopes and fears, trust and mistrust, resulted from physically removing ourselves from our tables and agenda. Years later I ask myself if this is what it means "to make room for the Holy Spirit."

It was a turning point. The many-years-long process resulted in finding a new direction that defined what these church bodies should do together, and what they needed to continue to do separately. It would take three more years to realize the outcomes of this meeting. As in all human endeavors, nothing turned out perfectly. The new directions were not without their naysayers. Controversy had not been eliminated, but we found a way to move forward.

The act of moving away from our tables, agendas, and predispositions into a circle of genuine conversation and prayer yielded results that "the power at work within us was able to accomplish abundantly far more than all we could ask or imagine" (cf. Eph 3:20).

Antoine de Saint-Exupéry said, "It is only with the heart that we can see rightly; what is essential is invisible to the eye." This seeing with the heart is authenticity for leaders—to be authentically human *and* mysteriously made in God's image, doing God's work.

—Jim Schrag of Newton, Kansas, has served as a pastor and as executive director of Mennonite Church USA.

A Dark Night

> O Lord, why do you cast me off?
> Why do you hide your face from me?
>
> —Psalm 88:14

We were at an impasse. For four years our church board had struggled to resolve our need for more space. Clearly we needed to do something. Our regular attendance was 130, and our sanctuary seated only 140.

We had not been ignoring the problem. In the last four years we had appointed five committees to discern future needs. We drafted mission and vision statements, experimented with two worship services, explored church planting, and had our property assessed. No matter what option was proposed, our congregation rejected them all.

In desperation the congregation considered forming a partnership with a neighboring congregation that had a large building but a small attendance. The plan was to sell our property, move in with them, and essentially become one congregation. But the membership rejected this option also.

We were clearly at an impasse. We had explored all the options we could imagine. We tried to pray, but it felt as though our words were falling to the ground like black walnuts and rolling into some forgotten ravine. Our corporate soul felt empty. We wanted God to give us direction, yet no guidance seemed forthcoming. God seemed far away, and in our lowest moments we even wondered if God cared for us. We were hopelessly stuck.

Now in retrospect I realize that our board was in a dark night. The dark night is a unique spiritual experience first named by John of the Cross (1542–91),[3] though it has occurred to God's people for thousands of years. It has three characteristics: an inability to pray as we have normally prayed, a general sense of spiritual dryness or abandonment, and a burning wish to sense God's presence and power. It can happen to individuals, boards, and even whole institutions. It may last for months or years.

The dark night is not God's punishment. Rather, it is a means by which God transforms us to become better Christians—more focused on God instead of other things, more dedicated to the mission of God, and more compassionate to others. It is a gift that eventually brings us more in line with what God intends to accomplish in our lives and in the world. Although it seems like an experience of darkness or obscurity, it is actually God's way of purifying and setting us on fire.

Our church board stayed in a dark night for most of a year. During that year, board members drew closer to each other and became more deeply committed to finding the good for our congregation. We sought Christ above all else. Our impasse was broken when a neighbor offered us a property next door to the church. This new possibility offered a pathway for moving forward out of the darkness into the light.

—Daniel P. Schrock is pastor of Berkey Avenue Mennonite Fellowship in Goshen, Indiana. He is also a spiritual director and author of *The Dark Night: A Gift of God.*

Faith in Trying Times

> Be gracious to me, O Lord, for to you do I cry all day long.
> Gladden the soul of your servant, for to you, O Lord, I lift
>   up my soul.
> For you, O Lord, are good and forgiving, abounding in
>   steadfast love to all who call on you.
> Give ear, O Lord, to my prayer; listen to my cry of supplication.
> In the day of my trouble I call on you, for you will answer me.
> —Psalm 86:3-7

A man found the cocoon of an emperor moth and took it home so he could watch the moth come out of the cocoon. One day a small opening appeared. The man sat and watched the moth as it struggled to force its body through that little hole.

Then it seemed to stop making any progress. Out of kindness, the man decided to help the moth. With a pair of scissors he snipped off the remaining bit of the cocoon so the moth could get out. Soon the moth emerged, but it had a swollen body and shriveled wings. The man continued to watch the moth, expecting that in time the wings would enlarge and expand to support the body, which would simultaneously contract to its proper size. Neither happened. In fact, that little moth spent the rest of its life crawling around with a swollen body and shriveled wings. It was never able to fly.

In his kindness the man didn't understand that the struggle required for the moth to get through the tiny opening of the cocoon was God's way of forcing fluid from the body into the wings, preparing the moth for flight once it achieved its freedom.

As the moth could only achieve freedom and flight as a result of struggling, so we, and the organizations we lead, too become all God intends us to be through struggle. Sometimes we wish God would remove our struggles and take away all the obstacles. But just as the man's good intentions crippled the emperor moth, so we would be stunted if God would remove obstacles from us.

In hard times, many boards face difficult circumstances and tough decisions. In Psalm 86 King David, Israel's CEO, expressed his distress—even fear for his life. We sense urgency as he expresses fourteen prayer requests in quick succession. As king, David had all the kingdom's resources (supplies, money, an army, and servants) at his command. In spite of who he was and what he had, he realized that his true deliverance could come only from God. Through this psalm, David taught that God is greater than all problems, people, and circumstances. It is beautifully summarized in verse 7: "In the day of my trouble I will call to you, for you will answer me."

Whatever difficulties, trials, or struggles we are facing today, we can cry out to God and trust that God will answer our call. Psalm 107 repeatedly says, "They cried to the LORD in their trouble, and he saved them from their distress."

—Ronald Shank is chaplain at Brook Lane, a mental-health organization in Hagerstown, Maryland.

Tested and Dancing

> Jesus, full of the Holy Spirit, left the Jordan and was led by
> the Spirit in the wilderness, where for forty days he was
> tempted by the devil. He ate nothing during those days,
> and at the end of them he was hungry.
> —Luke 4:1-2 NIV

Have you been in the wilderness? Has your organization faced a major disappointment, a tough leadership transition, a conflict among board members?

Consider the experience of Gislaine, a Haitian immigrant in New York City working two jobs, earning $20,000 a year as a school-bus matron and an office cleaner. After the January 12, 2010, earthquake struck Haiti, she became desperate to stretch her small income to care for her three children, ages ten to fourteen. They were back in Port-au-Prince, living in the street by the front door of their demolished home. They could not go to school because it was destroyed, and now the rainy season was starting. Truly Gislaine was in the wilderness.

In the early ministry of Jesus, a series of events took place in the wilderness, as recounted in Luke 4:1-13. The temptation that Jesus faced in the wilderness was not a box of chocolates. Temptation was a major test, which came right after his baptism, when he had publicly declared his commitment to God's mission for his life. Jesus' response to the devil was to declare to the tester and to himself that God was at the center of his life and work.

What happens when our time of testing comes? It's not easy to lead an organization with integrity. The challenges of life's wilderness threaten to distract us from working for the big picture of peace and justice and the mending of creation.

When we're facing the test, we may not find it easy to allow God to lead us. In her book *The Unmistakable Touch of Grace*, Cheryl Richardson tells of a dream in which she heard dance music. She was approached by a God-figure who invited her to dance. Her partner urged her, "Relax and surrender to the music. Be patient as you learn. And take pleasure in the dance." As she and her partner moved with the music, she realized that she was receiving a glimpse of the creative process. She surrendered and become entranced by the flow of the dance. The dream ended, and she awoke feeling hopeful about her future.

When we are tested, our challenge is to trust in our divine dance partner. The ability to surrender is a sign of spiritual maturity. When we resist what comes from God, we experience suffering. When we are firmly wrapped around a desire, our peace of mind and happiness are held hostage by an obsessive need to control the outcome, says Richardson.

By faith we let go of how we think things should be and accept them as they are. It doesn't mean that we throw up our hands and do nothing. It means that we pay closer attention to the leading of our divine dance partner. Once we've done what we can, reaching out to those who have the resources to give us solid support, we let go and allow God to take over and bring about the result that will serve our spiritual development.

That's what Gislaine did when she met with an immigration attorney at Lutheran Social Services. Gislaine reached out to her landlady, who was making $77,000 a year and offered to cosponsor Gislaine's application to bring the children to New York. Gislaine took off valuable hours from work to fill out forms and gather documents.

It's uncertain what will be the outcome for the well-being of those children stuck in the rain-filled streets all day. But clearly the way out of the wilderness will be easier because of the contributions of Gislaine's landlady, her church, Lutheran Social Service, and Mennonite Central Committee (which serves Haitians in New York). Gislaine's attitude is open, trusting, surrendered. She is dancing to the music with her divine dance partner.

—Sylvia E. Shirk of New York City is pastor of Manhattan Mennonite Fellowship.

New Ways to Be the Hands of Christ

> Do not fear, for I have redeemed you;
> I have summoned you by name; you are mine.
> When you pass through the waters, I will be with you;
> and when you pass through the rivers, they will not sweep
>   over you.
> When you walk through the fire, you will not be burned;
> the flames will not set you ablaze.
> For I am the LORD your God, the Holy One of Israel, your Savior.
> —Isaiah 43:1b-3a NIV

One of my favorite stories on facing and surmounting disappointment is one I heard many years ago. In a small town in Italy, after World War II, townspeople gathered in the village piazza around their beloved statue of Christ, which had stood there for hundreds of years. Bombs from the recent war had devastated the villagers' lives. The blasts had decapitated their statue of Christ and blown off the arms. On this day they gathered around their Christ figure, which had once stood with arms outstretched—a gesture of love and protection over the village. Now the statue was headless and armless, a visual reminder of their own devastation and brokenness.

The villagers gathered to find ways to reconstruct their beloved Christ figure. Eventually a wise villager said, "It is right to replace the head of Christ on our statue. But instead of also replacing the arms and hands, perhaps the statue of Christ in our piazza should stand as a daily reminder that each one of us are the hands of Christ in our world today."

The villagers were deeply touched. And to this day the residents of this small town are reminded daily that they themselves are the hands of Christ in our broken world.

Sometimes disappointment overwhelms us and seems all-consuming, leaving us with little energy to move forward. But what would happen if, when there appears to be little hope, we can somehow begin to see ourselves as the hands of Christ in a new way, even amid our disappointments and brokenness? How might we, like the villagers, build something beautiful out of the pain and destruction around us?

When our Bridge of Hope affiliate staff and board gathered at our annual conference in October 2005, Hurricane Katrina was fresh on our minds. Our shared mission of ending homelessness for women and children by equipping churches to respond through mentoring friendship seemed more critical than ever. The hurricane was a devastating reminder of how much work was needed. Many of us felt discouraged and immobilized. In the face of such devastation and in light of the many more families facing homelessness, could we really make a difference? The idea of ending homelessness (our very mission) felt further from reality than ever.

As we talked about the devastation caused by the hurricane, we considered the story of the Christ statue. Together we began to reflect on new ways to be the hands of Christ. In the process, a renewed commitment and vision emerged in our midst. Within a year and a half our small network of Bridge of Hope affiliates had doubled from six to twelve locations.

Can you name a discouraging time your organization has faced recently? How might God be at work even now to redeem your disappointment, turning it into an opportunity for being the hands of Christ in your world?

—Edith Yoder is executive director of Bridge of Hope National, a Christian faith-based nonprofit whose vision is to end and prevent homelessness for women and children across the United States by calling churches into action.

Though Adversity May Befall Us

> Though the fig tree does not blossom, and no fruit is on
>   the vines;
> though the produce of the olive fails, and the fields yield
>   no food;
> though the flock is cut off from the fold, and there is no
>   herd in the stalls,
> yet I will rejoice in the Lord; I will exult in the God of my
>   salvation.
> God, the Lord, is my strength;
> he makes my feet like the feet of a deer, and makes me tread
>   upon the heights.
> —Habakkuk 3:17-19

Can we have faith in God when things go bad? Habakkuk writes these words amid serious difficulty in the kingdom of Judah. It was a difficult time, *and* yet Habakkuk affirms faith in the God of the covenant.

As any organizational leader knows, things don't always go according to plan. Organizations have their hills and valleys. Only those able to navigate the lows can have the joys of celebrating the highs.

I was chairman of the ministerial association to plan a citywide evangelistic crusade. At one meeting a lay leader thought I was not giving strong enough leadership and took over the meeting. As I left the session, I felt that I had failed. The evangelistic crusade went forward, but I had been deposed as chair.

Life has its disappointments. One child makes good grades, and another is a slow learner. Some parents know the pain of a handicapped son or daughter. Organizations face plateaus despite diligent efforts by the board and staff. A major fundraising effort may come up short, or a significant employee resigns. A board may reject the chair's leadership. How should leaders respond when faced with a major disappointment?

First, a careful analysis should be made of what went wrong and why. Leaders must have the humility to accept responsibility for what went wrong. In the illustration above, was my leadership inadequate? Or was my unauthorized successor unduly aggressive? Each person must accept their part in a failure and not be quick to point the accusing finger. Failure and disappointment are an unavoidable part of organizational life. Leaders should avoid groveling in a disappointment, but neither should they live in denial.

Second, analyze what went wrong and why. Was the timing wrong? Was the implementation faulty? Or was it a bad idea to begin with? Did the involved parties exercise due diligence in testing the proposal? Was the decision based on carefully collected and analyzed information?

And third, ask, "What can be learned from this disappointment?" Pain can bring gain for those willing to learn from it. A good leader does not get stuck in disappointment and hurt feelings, but turns the disappointment into a learning experience and applies that learning in the following days. It is possible to turn adversity into strength by asking, "What am I learning about myself? What am I learning about management and leadership? When am I learning from other people?"

In summary, quality, mature leaders face disappointment for what it is, own their part in it, learn from it, and move on.

This is where the *yets* of life come in. Habakkuk's faith did not waver in the God of the covenant. Job said, "Though He slay me, yet will I trust Him" (Job 13:15 NKJV). God does not abandon us when things go bad. Often God comes to us through others who walk with us through the valleys of disappointment and failure.

When Anna L. Barbauld wrote the song *Praise to God Immortal Praise* in 1772, she included four verses taken from the Habakkuk passage quoted above.[4] We do well to sing those verses when we go about our board service. Though adversity may befall me, yet will I rejoice in the Lord!

—Paul M. Zehr of Lancaster, Pennsylvania, has served as a Mennonite bishop, Bible teacher, and administrator.

Prayers

God who promises never to leave or forsake us,
 you invite us to cast all our cares on you.
Like a loving parent who comforts a child in distress,
 you long to console us when we are confused or afraid.
And so because we trust in you,
 we come today with troubled hearts
 and name our concern to you:
[*State the concern explicitly; don't just refer to it generically.*]

We admit that we're worried.
The ground beneath us seems to have shifted,
 and we aren't sure how to respond.
We're concerned about our public reputation,
 but even more, we're anxious about those who depend upon us,
 our employees and those whom we serve.
We feel threatened, confused, and disheartened.

Strengthen us, God, in the midst of trouble.
Protect us from hopelessness and despair.
Make us resilient as we face adversity.
Keep our faith strong,
 and help us to remember that you are the one
 who brings life out of death.

Grant us courage as we meet together
and face our disappointment.
Renew our hope in you and in one another
 as together we confront an uncertain future.
Let us glimpse some signs of your grace at work.

We pray in the name of Jesus, the Risen One,
 who promises to be with us always. Amen.

—Marlene Kropf is associate professor of spiritual formation and worship, Associated Mennonite Biblical Seminary, and the former denominational minister of worship for Mennonite Church USA.

We gather in your name, Creator God, to name our hurts and our failures. This is a sad time, a scary time, and even an embarrassing time. Yet we call on you to be present in the life of [*name of the organization, church, nonprofit*] with your healing power and compassionate love.
[*Option: Pause to allow for sentence prayers naming disappointments.*]

See our tears—and turn them into renewing waters.
Feel our aching hearts—and transform them into loving energy.
Touch our wounded spirits—and empower them for creating hope.
Forgive our mistakes—and renew us for meaningful service.
Hear our prayer, gracious God.
Amen.

—Dorothy Nickel Friesen has spent her professional career in the English classroom as a teacher and the last twenty-eight years as a Mennonite pastor, seminary administrator, and conference minister.

Loving God, be near to us in these days. Not everything we had hoped for, planned for, even worked for has met our expectations or yours. Yet we know that you love us still, need us still, and will use us still. On this day, we count on you to pick us up, dust us off, and plant our feet on higher ground. Amen.

—David Johnson Rowe is copastor of Greenfield Hill Congregational Church, Fairfield, Connecticut.

7

Meditations When Contemplating a Major Decision

Waiting in the Light, *Bob Anderson*
Faith to Navigate Change, *Wilma Ann Bailey*
A Backup When the Backup Fails, *R. Lee Delp*
Vision-Driven to Do God's Work, *Christopher J. Doyle*
Boldness for God, *Linda C. Fuller*
Know Your Story, *Nancy R. Heisey*
Honi and the Carob Tree, *Beryl Jantzi*
When Parting with a CEO Becomes Necessary, *Gerald W. Kaufman*
A Fragile and Gossamer Thread, *Jonathan P. Larson*
Making Room for Youthful Dreamers, *Albert C. Lobe*
Claiming God's Promises, *Wilmer Martin*
Seeing Opportunity in Recession, *Larry D. Miller*
God Chose Us, *Don Mosley*
Holding to the Standards of Justice, Mercy, and Humility, *Jonathan T. M. Reckford*
Beyond the Valley of the Now, *Terry Shue*
Following the Servant Jesus in Volatile Times, *Tom Sine*
In Change There Is Opportunity, *David Snell*
Faith Stories Build Community, *Karl C. Sommers*
Treasure in Clay Jars, *Karl C. Sommers*
Scaling Mountains, *Edgar Stoesz*
Risking for Success, *Edgar Stoesz*
Whom Shall I Fear? *Sharon and Anne Waltner*

How Does a Christian Organization Plan? *David Williams*
Discerning the Future and the Calling, *David M. Wine*
Prayers

Introduction

Great boards are distinguished by their ability to discern and make
wise decisions. Should they approve an entirely new service line
or enter a quite different market or constituency group? Should
they entertain an affiliation, merger, or acquisition? How should
they lay off staff to survive a recession? How should they process
a leadership transition they are facing? Such excruciating decisions
can rattle the organization to its very core and call into question its
reason for being.

Board work is about the future, and the future is uncertain. In
the words of Robert Greenleaf, "The leader needs to have a *sense
of the unknowable* and be able to *foresee the unforeseeable*."[1]
This calls for drawing on spiritual resources.

Times of crisis are also times of opportunity. The Chinese
proverb states it well. "Crisis = danger/opportunity." Danger and
opportunity should be seen as two sides of the same coin: they go
together. By its very nature, opportunity is accompanied by danger.
Opportunity is denied to those who are unable or unwilling to risk
the danger associated with it. Caution is not always the best course
of action. This is often hard for governing boards, whose instincts
are often more conservative and cautious about the protection of
assets. Hear these words from various sources:

> *Put me to the test, says the* LORD *of hosts; see if I will not
> open the windows of heaven for you and pour down for
> you an overflowing blessing.*
> —Malachi 3:10

> *You see things; and you say, "Why?" But I dream things
> that never were; and I say, "Why not?"*
> —George Bernard Shaw, in *Back to Methuselah*, part 1, act 1

*We should attempt things so great that they are doomed
to failure unless God intervenes.*
        —Henry Blackaby, in *Experiencing God*[2]

*There is nothing more difficult to take in hand, more per-
ilous to conduct, or more uncertain in its success, than to
take the lead in the introduction of a new order of things.
Because the innovator has for enemies all those who
have done well under the old conditions, and lukewarm
defenders in those who may do well under the new.*
        —Niccolo Machiavelli, in *The Prince*, chapter 6

Frankly, boards do not have a map to navigate them through
treacherous waters. If there were such, there would be little need
for discernment. Boards are composed of human beings who
always "see through a glass, darkly" (1 Cor 13:12 KJV). However,
we assert that God's Spirit can serve as a kind of global-positioning
system. The following meditations offer insight into how spiritual
resources can offer orientation and direction when boards face
major decisions.

Select a meditation from this chapter that speaks best to the
situation facing you. Feel free to inject your thoughts and adapt it
to your circumstance. Conclude with one of the prayers that follow, again feeling free to add to it and adapt it. Some may want
to repeat the Lord's Prayer in unison or sing a song together. Use
silence and thoughtful pauses. Be relaxed and worshipful. Make
it your goal to set a spiritual tone that will pervade the entire
meeting.

Waiting in the Light

> But if we hope for what we do not see, we wait for it with
> patience.
> —Paul, in Romans 8:25

"In the Light wait, where unity is." This is the counsel that George Fox, the first Quaker, gave his followers. It remains sound advice today, especially for a retirement community, like ours, embarking on a search for a successor to a long-serving and beloved executive director.

Fox's advice was countercultural in seventeenth century, and it is still countercultural today. In times of potential anxiety, such as searching for a new leader, our culture transmits a message grounded in a need for immediate control and certainty: "Don't just sit there: do something." The Quaker way instead says: "Don't just do something: sit there." Wait in the Light.

As we begin our search, then, we turn toward the Light. The Light is within each of us individually and among all of us collectively. When we live in that Light, our deepest values accord with our every action. At the outset of this search, we pause to give great thanks for the Light as we have experienced it through the integrity and caring of our current leader and in the vibrant life together of our community under her leadership. Putting aside our individual egos, we open ourselves up to the assurance that the Light will illuminate our collective path throughout the search process. Caressed by this Light, we become calm and centered as well as conscientious in all we plan and do. Our searching proceeds from our purpose, not our anxiety.

Waiting is next. Waiting in the Light is not for the fainthearted or intellectually timid. It is an active discipline, not a passive mindset. The discipline of waiting resists the urge for immediate and comfortable answers, instead letting the Light search our minds and our hearts and lead us in a full and honest exploration of our fears and hopes, our weaknesses and strengths, our challenges and opportunities.

The way of waiting depends on a carefully planned and patient process and trusts that wisdom will emerge through continuing revelation, close listening, collective discernment, and widespread participation in identifying the nature and needs of the community and the desirable attributes of our next executive director. A search process must be endured and can be enjoyed, but it should not be rushed. It takes time, a disciplined approach, and a patient spirit to appreciate and absorb the leadings of the Light and the wisdom of the community.

Unity comes at the end of Fox's sentence. The board of directors is the group legally and solely responsible for hiring an executive director; in a narrow sense, then, unity can be understood as all board members agreeing on the choice of a new leader. But in a broader and deeper sense, unity means a congruence between Light and leadership. This congruence is between the values of our community and the integrity and leadership capabilities of the person who will next guide us. Fox assures us that our end of unity is already and always present in our beginning, in the Light. If we will simply still ourselves while waiting in the Light, we will make the connection and find the congruence.

"In the Light wait, where unity is."

—Bob Anderson of Newtown, Pennsylvania, has worked with the Quaker-related retirement community Pennswood Village.

Faith to Navigate Change

> Do not be afraid.
>
> —Jesus, in Matthew 14:27

In Matthew's account of Jesus' walking on the water during a storm (Matt 14:22-33), Peter models courage when he asks Jesus to summon him to walk on the water toward him. When Jesus complies by calling Peter to come, he courageously starts walking on the water. But midway he turns his attention from Jesus to the storm raging around him. He falters. He sinks into the sea. Then Jesus takes him by the hand and prevents him from drowning.

This remarkable story should challenge boards to take bold steps in a new direction and sometimes-uncharted waters, making changes to assure the survival, growth, and continued viability of an institution.

Although this story is often used as a model of failure, it is far from that. Peter demonstrates that he is willing to try something new that requires a lot of courage. Jesus encourages him to take a chance. As a result, he experiences something that the other disciples do not. Like Jesus, Peter walks on the water.

When a year-old child stands erect and takes her first tentative steps, we do not ridicule her for her failure to cross the room. We praise her for her new accomplishment. She will fall many times before she masters the technique. But she would not walk at all if she were afraid to take the first step.

As long as Peter keeps his eyes on Jesus, his steps are sure. But when he becomes distracted by the storm, he starts to sink. Jesus rescues him. This demonstrates that Jesus is concerned about the safety, health, and well-being of Peter's physical body, not just his spiritual state. So Jesus saves him by grabbing hold of him and preventing him from drowning. Here Peter has another experience that the other disciples do not. He feels the touch of Jesus.

Jesus affirms that Peter has faith. He just does not have enough faith. This is a growth area for him. But Peter's little bit of faith was enough to give him the courage to step into uncertain territory and transform the theology of the disciples. According to Matthew, they proclaim Jesus to be the Son of God. Would they have received this insight without Peter's courageous step onto the raging waters and then Jesus' rescue?

Board meetings are often routine. There are approvals to be made, reports to be heard, and questions to be asked and answered. But every board comes to a point where it has to make significant changes, and every significant change is a step into the unknown. Perhaps it has to choose a new leader. Perhaps it has to make difficult financial decisions. Perhaps it has to say yes or no to new or old programs.

Every institution has to change to grow and remain viable, because the world around it is in a constant state of flux. Change always brings with it uncertainties. Change often makes some people uncomfortable. It is easy to become distracted by the "What ifs . . . ?" Change is always accompanied by uncertainty until the new structure, people, or programs are in place and functioning. Institutions are a means by which the will of God is actualized, but only if the institution keeps its eyes on its divine purpose and calling.

—Wilma Ann Bailey of Indianapolis, Indiana, is professor of Hebrew and Aramaic Scripture at Christian Theological Seminary.

A Backup When the Backup Fails

The LORD will keep your going out and your coming in
from this time on and for evermore.
—Psalm 121:8

The funeral lasted two hours, but it felt like just minutes. The church meeting room was packed. Friends and business acquaintances far outnumbered the family. It was a diverse gathering of people, mourning the loss of a forty-one-year-old husband, son, father, cousin, brother, nephew, business associate, and friend.

Eighteen months earlier the president and CEO announced his retirement. Forty-five years was enough. His son was the logical successor. The family was certain that with his good education and twenty-plus years with the business, he was ready. I was responsible as board chair to ensure a smooth transition. At the son's insistence, a search committee was appointed. Other candidates were considered, but Jack was the clear choice. The board, shareholders, and employees were pleased. We had our leader, we thought, for the next generation. We felt blessed.

Two months into the new position, Jack casually informed me that he was experiencing some stomach discomfort and had seen his doctor. It didn't seem to be anything major, but the discomfort turned into distress and went on for months. Doctors thought it was stomach ulcers. Soon it was evident that it had to be something else. Extensive testing revealed that Jack had stomach cancer. The news was devastating for everyone. His father was unable to resume the leadership during this terrible time of hospitalization, treatment, and desperate search to save his son's life.

It was clear that the board needed to make another provision to fill the breach. We put our grief aside and devised a plan with the management and employees. We honored Jack by keeping him up to date and getting his input. Jack did all he could to be involved. In "The President's Corner" of the newsletter, Jack wrote:

> Often change is dictated by our circumstances. In a sense we
> are forced to change in order to continue to have positive
> outcomes. Change is not always what we want or the way
> we want it, but it is what it is. In other words, as life's cir-

cumstances change, we must learn to work within the framework of the new reality. In my personal case, I have had to spend most of my energy recently on regaining my health. This was definitely not in my plan for 2004. I believe if you look to the future with hope and optimism and act with enthusiasm, we will meet our goals and more.

With prayer, unity of purpose, commitment, and leadership, our company survived this harrowing and unanticipated experience. By drawing on abilities and goodwill in our ranks, we were able to survive when even our backup plan failed.

On occasions, boards are confronted by challenges for which there is no road map. This tests the strength of their relationships, their maturity, their resolve, and their creativity. With faith they are able to bring beauty from ashes as they draw on spiritual resources to find passage through the storm and end up the stronger for it!

—R. Lee Delp of Lansdale, Pennsylvania, has worked in profit and nonprofit boardrooms for many years.

Vision-Driven to Do God's Work

> "For I know the plans I have for you," declares the LORD,
> "plans to prosper you and not to harm you,
> plans to give you hope and a future."
> —Jeremiah 29:11 NIV

Organizations need a clear and compelling vision to guide their planning. The Bible even tells us that "where there is no vision, the people perish" (Prov 29:18 KJV). Directors spend hours wrestling with mission and vision statements, wanting to get them just right. Sometimes the needed change comes with new leadership.

Directors need to deliberately seek God's leading when defining their mission and vision. They need to ask, "What does God want us to do?" Though history is important, an organization needs to spend far more time looking to the future. Kierkegaard wrote, "Life must be understood backward. But then . . . it must be lived forward."[3] Organizational leadership can be likened to an automobile that has a large windshield, permitting us to see where we are going, but only a small mirror to see where we have been.

During my years as CEO of American Leprosy Missions (ALM), we talked much about vision and mission. The leprosy world was undergoing significant changes. A cure for leprosy was discovered in the early 1980s, resulting in a worldwide push to get the drugs to the patients. The numbers of new cases and patients under care dropped dramatically. We asked ourselves, "Is there still need for ALM, or should we be inventing a new future for ourselves?"

During a weekend retreat, the board wrestled hard and long to come up with a statement that would define ALM's future activities. Mission, we reminded ourselves, is what we are doing presently while vision is looking down the road to identify what we want to become. Vision is what God wants us to do and become to serve people and create a better world.

Our discussion started on a note of idealism, but soon we were down to choosing the right wording, some of which had little to do with who we were and what we meant to accomplish. When it appeared as though our day would end without coming to an agreement, one member spoke out in frustration. While packing his papers to make a dash for the airport, he cut through all the verbiage and said, "Aren't we trying to complete the task of eradicating leprosy? Then why don't we simply say we are God's servants, trying to free the world from leprosy?"

That was it, and everyone in the room knew it instantly! Christ was substituted for God, and we had our statement: "Christ's servants, freeing the world from leprosy." It gave our work focus for the next decade.

Boards need to work together, pray together, and inspire each other to excellence. They need to engage each other vigorously until they arrive at their best conclusion. Without a vision, an organization is adrift or busy with all the same old things. A vision can rally the organization and point it in a solid direction.

Does your organization have a vision that is clear and challenging? Does it permeate the whole organization and influence your board and management decision making?

—Christopher J. Doyle of Greenville, South Carolina, is executive director of African Enterprise and earlier was president and CEO of American Leprosy Missions.

Boldness for God

> The saddest summary of a life contains three descriptions:
> "Could have, might have, and should have."
> —Louis E. Boone[4]

We can imagine that Boone's parents were procrastinators. He might have been a frustrated child who often wanted to do things, but . . . for whatever reason, it didn't happen. His intentions were good, but the follow-through was weak. So he developed a mantra to excuse his lack of performance.

Boone's quote applies to organizations as well as individuals. I wonder how many trustees have looked back and said to themselves, "We could have done thus and so?" Or, "We might have, we should have!" Regrets!

I have no memory of many meetings the Habitat for Humanity International board conducted during the twenty-nine years my beloved and late husband, Millard, and I were in the leadership. The ones I remember are when Millard did something extraordinary to convince fellow board members to accept his bold initiatives. When wanting to demonstrate how important something was to him, Millard on occasions literally jumped on the boardroom table to make his case.

Millard liked to take advantage of Habitat milestones to spread the word and raise much-needed funds to build more houses. For Habitat's seventh anniversary in 1983, we sponsored a 700-mile walk from Americus, Georgia, to Indianapolis. Our goal was to raise $100,000 above regular giving. It was unorthodox, to say the least, but it succeeded.

By the time of our tenth anniversary, Millard proposed a goal of $10 million. He liked the sound of it: Ten million to celebrate the tenth anniversary. The board was shocked beyond words. Nothing in past giving trends suggested that such an ambitious goal was possible. Millard was buoyed by the fact that President Jimmy Carter had recently joined the board and assumed that his fame, in addition to his own optimism, would carry the day.

After more than an hour of deliberations, Millard jumped on the table, literally! While everyone was in shock to see six-foot four-inch Millard on the board table, President Carter said, "Look, if we set a goal of $10 million, we may not raise every penny. However, we will most likely raise more than if we set a lower goal." That reasoning seemed to make sense, and coming from a former president of the United States didn't hurt the cause. Wonder of wonders, the entire $10 million was raised.

Guess what the challenge was for the twelfth anniversary? This time the board was more supportive!

Are there bold goals or initiatives that "could have, would have, and should have" been realized but never happened? Rather than stepping out on faith, have you seen a bold idea become assigned to an ad hoc committee where it languished and died? Millard's favorite Bible verse was "Ye have not, because ye ask not!" (James 4:2 KJV).

Millard had an amazing sense of what would work. He knew his capabilities and had faith in the ability of others. His boldness empowered others. He often invited listeners to imagine a line drawn on the ground. "On one side," said Millard, "is faith; on the other, foolishness. God wants us to get as close to the foolishness line as we can without crossing over. With God, all things are possible. All things may not be easy, but with God, all things are possible!" I have witnessed this kind of bold faith over and over, resulting in amazing successes to the glory of God.

—Linda C. Fuller of Americus, Georgia, is cofounder of Habitat for Humanity International and also cofounder of The Fuller Center for Housing.

Know Your Story

> For I handed on to you as of first importance what I in turn
>   had received:
>   that Christ died for our sins in accordance with the
>   scriptures,
>   and that he was buried,
>   and that he was raised on the third day in accordance
>   with the scriptures,
>   and that he appeared to Cephas, then to the twelve.
> —Paul, in 1 Corinthians 15:3-5

When the Mennonite World Conference General Council gathered in 2006, on the agenda was a second reading of the Statement of Shared Convictions, a brief document outlining theological understandings that shape the identity of the about one hundred Anabaptist-related associations of member churches in nations around the world. The process of coming to the draft statement had taken nearly ten years: it had included gathering confessions of faith of particular member churches, circulating and studying drafts in many parts of the world, and late-night sessions of a drafting committee representing the five continental regions.

One of the most important parts of the statement was how it articulated beliefs about Jesus Christ, the collection of understandings that most clearly ties Anabaptist-related churches to all other Christians. Centuries of debate and development of creedal statements were behind us, but among us were also delegates from contemporary churches that witness to faith in Christ in a multitude of interreligious settings. We struggled with the wording.

Suddenly I was overwhelmed with the sense that all those Christians down through the ages who had debated and argued over who Jesus was for them were in the room with us. I couldn't see them, but they were present—and rather than taking sides in our discussion, they were cheering us on, encouraging us to find a good way to talk about Jesus in our statement.

I intervened in the discussion and told the delegate body about my experience. Shortly afterward we took a lunch break, and when we returned, we were able to agree on the wording of our statement: "Jesus is the Son of God. Through his life and teachings, his cross and resurrection, he showed us how to be faithful disciples, redeemed the world, and offers eternal life."

As a historian of early Christianity, I had access to specialized information about early christological debates, which may have contributed to my experience. Yet already when the apostle Paul wrote to the Corinthians, he underlined how important it is for *all* believers to know their own story. In his famous chapter on the resurrection, he begins with what many scholars call an early confession of faith. He shares this confession, not as abstract principle, but in the form of story, handing down the tradition he received from one generation to the next.

At the heart of the Christian faith is a story—the story of Scripture, the story of the life of Jesus, and the story of those who lived and walked with Jesus and then carried that story to the world. To make sense of the hard questions, Paul says, "Let's start with our own story."

Boards face many challenging decisions: selecting the right leader(s) for their staff, assuring that all their stakeholders are represented, shaping and reviewing policies that release the creative energy of their programs without sacrificing accountability. Remembering the organization's own founding stories can help.

I learned from our experiences in the Mennonite World Conference General Council that making a space for diverse stories is also critical. We didn't focus on our differences, but we allowed them to be articulated and woven into our conversation. Our common desire to express God's love through the churches provided the web that held us together. Likewise, the story of your board's mission can flourish while honoring the different gifts each one brings to the table.

—Nancy R. Heisey of Harrisonburg, Virginia, is undergraduate academic dean at Eastern Mennonite University and served as moderator of Mennonite World Conference in 2003–9.

Honi and the Carob Tree

> Happy are those who . . . are like trees planted by streams
> of water,
> which yield their fruit in its season, and their leaves do not
> wither.
> In all that they do, they prosper.
> —Psalm 1:1, 3

I am a fan of Jewish writings and literature. Over the centuries, rabbis have taught through story. Perhaps this influenced Jesus' teaching style and use of parable. Organizations need storytellers as well. These are people who remember and retell the narrative of an organization's mission and purpose. To be true to our past and successful in moving forward, we need to have periodic reminders from where we have come and the principles on which our organizations were founded.

The Talmud has a revered place in Jewish culture. It is a record of Jewish thought, stating who they are as a people and what they are called to do and be. One story I have grown to appreciate is "Honi and the Carob Tree." As a young boy, Honi was out walking when he saw an old man planting a carob tree. After watching him for several minutes, Honi asked, "How long will it be before the tree bears fruit?" "It will be many years," said the old man. "Do you expect to ever taste the fruit of the tree?" asked Honi. "Probably not," said the old man. "Then why bother?" asked Honi.

The old man replied that when he was a boy, he was able to enjoy the fruit of trees that were planted by his father and grandfather. Now he feels that it is his responsibility to plant trees for future generations to enjoy.

We are called to recognize that we also reap what others have sown. Out of a grateful spirit, we are called to sow seeds and plant trees that we may never harvest so that future generations can benefit from our having been on this earth.

A question that all directors should ask themselves at least annually is this: "What do we want to see outlive our involvement with this organization? What legacy will we leave behind? Are we making progress toward that goal?"

Making the world a better place may seem like a lofty goal. Maybe we should bring that idea closer to home. Psalm 1 calls us to bear fruit right where we are planted. Some may be called on to branch out and make a global influence. But most of us are called to serve right where we are planted, in our neighborhoods and in our places of work. The streams that have nurtured us are where we can best give back and bear fruit.

My goal in life is not so much to change the world as it is to live a life that expresses and manifests a spirit of gratitude. This gratitude must be shown not only with mere words but especially in action—such as planting trees. A mature tree provides the gift of fruit to be enjoyed here and now. The fruit of the trees I plant will benefit persons I may never meet, even as I have benefited from the work and forethought of others. If that happens, I will be truly joyful as I end my lifework in this world!

—Beryl Jantzi of Harrisonburg, Virginia, is a pastor and directs stewardship education for Everence, a financial and mutual aid organization.

When Parting with a CEO Becomes Necessary

> Barnabas wanted to take with them John called Mark. But Paul
> decided not to take with them one who had deserted them in
> Pamphylia and had not accompanied them in the work. The
> disagreement became so sharp that they parted company.
> —Luke's report, in Acts 15:37-39

This story from one of the early missionary journeys reveals the human side of our early leaders. It may surprise us that these godly persons actually lost their tempers, and that the conflict between Paul and Barnabas was so personal that they chose to leave on separate boats. Paul had a reputation for being temperamental. And even though Barnabas was known to be a good mediator, he and Paul were unable to work out their differences.

A modern-day leadership equivalent may be the relationship between the chief executive officer (CEO) and the board chair. Often that relationship works well, and the mission is accomplished. Occasionally, though, that doesn't happen, and we depart on separate boats. As Christians, we should be able to find better ways of handling our differences.

It begins by being more skillful at selecting our CEOs. Although it's impossible to know how an executive will perform on the job, we should do better assessments during the hiring process. Second, are we asking the right questions and getting honest and complete references? Sometimes boards are in a hurry because the need is imminent or because of our own busy schedules. Sometimes it is wise to engage a professional search firm.

Once the CEO is hired, it is important for the board to monitor the CEO's performance. The chair and the CEO should meet regularly to insure that the CEO is on the same page with the board and to provide affirmation where it is deserved. Always the basis of such ongoing evaluations is the written job description. The CEO should not be in doubt as to one's standing. The board and the CEO should listen carefully to each other and work together and resolve difference as they arise.

Occasionally, in spite of the best intentions, it becomes necessary for the CEO to be terminated. If proper dialogue has gone on between the board and the CEO, termination should not come as a surprise; it should have been preceded by ample opportunity to correct what is not satisfactory. Ideally, separation is by mutual consent. Such CEOs can then move on to another assignment more in keeping with their gifts.

Paul and John Mark, we remember, eventually got back together, and both continued to play an important role in the expanding Christian church (cf. 2 Tim 4:11). If boards and their administrators part, one hopes both will grow from the experience. In contrast with Paul and Barnabas, tempers don't have to flare, and sometimes differences can be resolved. If separation still seems necessary, it is best for it to happen in the spirit of Christian love—blessing each other for the new journeys.

The selection, supervision, and support of the CEO are the board's most important function. It is through the CEO that the board's responsibilities are put into practice. When it is discovered that the CEO is not the right person for the job, it is important for termination to be done lovingly and sensitively. If the board has carried out its responsibilities properly, both will eventually be able to be fellow missionaries like Paul and Barnabas—even if on separate boats.

—Gerald W. Kaufman of Akron, Pennsylvania, has been a clinical social worker and is author of *Monday Marriage*.

A Fragile and Gossamer Thread

> Since we live by the Spirit, let us keep in step with the Spirit.
> —Paul, in Galatians 5:25 NIV

It is not unusual for things to be severed from their root. Take the common parting words "Goodbye." At their origin, it was the archaic expression, "God be with ye." Over the course of generations, like some stone tumbling in a mountain stream, it became smoothed and rounded. And over time, any trace of its original significance slipped away: it has ceased to be a blessing and has become the husk of a ritual at parting.

On a much larger scale, the acids of our time have slowly leached away the awareness of a spiritual dimension, as the dazzle of the material world takes captive the eyes and imaginations of our day. Even those of us who profess faith in something beyond that world find ourselves living like our secular neighbors, like practical agnostics. It is difficult to avoid being severed from those spiritual moorings in our workaday lives, or in the leadership we bring to "doing good."

A traditional tale from Scandinavia points to the danger of the drift we suffer when we go with that cultural flow. Somewhere in a great barn a spider was busy with what such creatures do: spinning a gossamer web. The architecture of the web was exquisite, its fine filaments falling into precise place, giving balance, strength, and symmetry to the whole. When the pattern was complete, the spider surveyed the work. It noticed a single filament attached to the center of the pattern and rising into the darkness of the rafters above. Forgetting its purpose, the spider came to see it as a clumsy error and so deftly severed that vertical thread.

The effect was immediate and pervasive. The entire pattern was lost. The web collapsed in on itself and lost its symmetry as well as its utility. What was once a work of integrity, natural beauty, and strength was reduced to a vain tangle.

That connection that "rises to the rafters far above" and holds the strength and beauty of the web intact is much more than a cursory prayer or moment of silence at the outset of deliberations. The connection is a way of being anchored, secured, grounded, and sustained. If after a brief curtsy in the direction of "the rafters," we proceed to transact our business out of self-seeking, sleight of hand, coercion, prejudice, or arrogance, no one can protect us from the collapse and disgrace that will follow. But that single, fragile filament that holds the pattern in place needs to be carried into each conversation, into each role we play, into each encounter, into speaking and listening, even into our silences. It is the lifeline of all lasting endeavors. It lends grace to the ordinary. It makes radiant the homely. It gives rhythm and order to the groping and faltering. And it makes fruitful what seems woefully meager.

Who dares to proceed without that filament? Who would take even the first step in making heaven's work our own without reaching for this defining and fragile strand? Let it master the whole pattern. Let it have pride of place in its beauty, symmetry, and strength.

For all who yearn for such things, there is a suitable and indispensable blessing: "God be with ye."

—Jonathan P. Larson of Atlanta, Georgia, is a pastor, writer, and storyteller.

Making Room for Youthful Dreamers

In the last days it will be, God declares,
that I will pour out my Spirit upon all flesh,
and your sons and your daughters shall prophesy,
and your young men shall see visions,
and your old men shall dream dreams.

—Peter, quoting Joel in Acts 2:17

Mennonite Central Committee sent Martha and me to India in 1964. We were seconded to the Bihar Mennonite Mission to administer an emergency relief program and a mission hospital. We were 22 years of age. A food-for-work program built and paid for 3 schools, 450 wells, and some 50 miles of road. On any given day we could receive 50 railway cars of rice, wheat, and oil for distribution to the laborers. Over the 3 years, the 14 small, tribal Mennonite congregations fed 4,000 nursing and pregnant mothers and older folks daily. What a difference the church made in the lives of those people, and in ours!

At an early age we had experienced what Frederick Buechner describes as the intersection between the world's deepest needs and our own inner gladness.[5] Our lives were changed forever!

By contrast, I am troubled by the hesitation I see in our present-day reluctance to entrust youth with heavy responsibilities. Everything has become so professionalized that the budding resource of youth no longer qualifies. If the applications we sent to the Mennonite Central Committee were to be received today, we would be told politely to get to the end of the line and earn our right to participate in a position of responsibility.

Years later, Mennonite Central Committee asked me to undertake a study to determine why the number of young adults volunteering for service was in such steep decline. Across Canada and the United States, young adults told me that they wanted to be taken seriously. They wanted to be free to ask questions. They wanted to be heard. Above all, they wanted to be trusted. "Survival," they said, "is an issue for older folks; young people like to be free to dream and think new thoughts, not just fit into inherited structures."

In Calcutta, I expressed my sense that idealism and patience were in short supply among young adults. James Hartley, a Fulbright scholar and professor of economics, listened and replied, "There is a certain self-loathing of America among both students and professors. . . . We are in a period of deconstruction."

A young Mennonite Central Committee worker in Bangladesh put it this way: "My generation has an ingrained and mortal fear of neocolonialism, of leaders who are old."

Juxtapose this impatience of youth with the idealism expressed in a July 18, 2007, *New York Times* report of "The Elders." Those named were people such as Desmond Tutu, Jimmy Carter, Nelson Mandela, Muhammad Yunus, Li Zhaoxing. They vowed to work both publicly and behind the scenes to support courage where there is fear, foster agreement where there is conflict, and inspire hope where there is despair.

What would happen if these "Elders" traveled to Zimbabwe and pressed Robert Mugabe to care for his people? Or sat at the Wailing Wall in Jerusalem and called for security for Israel and land for Palestinians? What if every undergraduate in Canada and the United States were encouraged to serve two years in a Peace Corp? What if we built 10,000 schools for girls in Afghanistan rather than sending 10,000 troops? What if our not-for-profit structures embodied the energy and passion of youth, the experience of age, the beauty of color, and knew no national boundaries?

Dreaming? As leaders we are called to be dreamers—both young and old, in tandem! Langston Hughes calls us to "hold fast to dreams," for without them life is "barren" and "frozen," grounded like a "broken-winged bird."[6] Real dreamers have their heads in the clouds and their feet on the ground.

—Albert C. Lobe of Kitchener, Ontario, is a veteran worker with Mennonite Central Committee, North America; representative to Mennonite World Conference; and board chair of Conrad Grebel University College.

Claiming God's Promises

> But the Lord said to me, "Do not say, 'I am only a boy';
> for you shall go to all to whom I send you, and you shall
> speak whatever I command you.
> Do not be afraid of them, for I am with you to deliver you,
> says the Lord."
>
> —Jeremiah 1:7-8

A TourMagination tour group was participating in worship in Jamaica. The church was packed with worshippers from Australia, Germany, United States, Canada, England, and Ireland. It was interesting to watch the international visitors react to a Jamaican worship service. One tour member was so touched that she removed her necklace and placed it on a beautiful Jamaican girl.

The sermon was by a member of the choir who appeared to be in his midteens. He asked people to turn with him to the book of Revelation. After he began to read, he realized that he had the wrong passage. Some parishioners were embarrassed for him. After awkwardly consulting his notes, he said, "Excuse me. I mean the Gospel of Matthew." He then read the correct passage, followed by a chorus of "Amens" and "Hallelujahs." Observing this, I was reminded of God's promise to Jeremiah, "Do not be afraid, . . . for I am with you to deliver you."

A few days later I was meditating on this Jeremiah text when I realized that this was the tenth anniversary of Habitat for Humanity Canada, an organization to which I had given my full energy as executive director and from which I had had a painful separation. It was a traumatic day for me. I had been going 120 miles per hour in pursuit of building houses with and for the poor, and then I hit a brick wall. I felt like a failure. I couldn't even say goodbye to my staff at the National Office or the Habitat affiliates and supporters across Canada, or staff and supporters in Jamaica.

In retrospect, I was glad that I had not accepted the counsel of some board members and colleagues who advised me to fight my termination. I recall with gratitude how my family and community of faith stood with me during those traumatic days. God used them to protect me from myself and to preserve my leadership gifts for the future.

Fear of the unknown and of the future can hinder our faith, but Jeremiah tells us, "Do not be afraid." Faith in God sustained me. During these long days and even longer nights, I had a mysterious sense that God was in control. I still question whether it was God's will for me to leave as I had and feel certain that it did not need to happen as it did. But I accepted it, and now I see how that closed door made me available for TourMagination, a ministry of building bridges among Christians and other faiths with custom-designed travel.

When we claim God's promises, we don't need to fear the future. Martin Luther King Jr. said, "Faith is taking the first step even when you don't see the whole staircase."

God's promises need to be claimed as we try to discern the future amid uncertainty. God's promises, when we appropriate them to our lives and believe them in our heart of hearts, protect and guide us.

—Wilmer Martin of Waterloo, Ontario, is owner and president of TourMagination and author of *Building Bridges*.

Seeing Opportunity in Recession

> For surely I know the plans I have for you, says the LORD,
> plans for your welfare and not for harm, to give you a
> future with hope.
> —Jeremiah 29:11

When the Mennonite Mutual Aid (MMA) board of directors met in February 2009, we were going through one of the most difficult economic recessions ever experienced in MMA's sixty-four-year history. Our investment management businesses were all suffering losses as we saw assets under management decline from a high of $1.9 billion to $1.4 billion. Locally in Elkhart County, Indiana, we were experiencing unemployment of 15 percent. To lessen the shock that the recession was having on the nation, President Obama visited our area to announce plans for a $787 billion economic stimulus program.

In the first day of our board meeting, we discussed financial risks and their impact on our business plans. We were thankful that MMA remained financially strong, but the uncertainties about the economy created fear and anxiety in our discussions.

The second day began with a meditation by our vice chair who, with the help of a PowerPoint presentation, shared stories and photos out of her life. As I saw the pictures of her family, school years, college friends, and local congregation, I thought about how my own life has been formed and shaped by my family, friends, and church. Carol's story included the many transitions we experience in following Christ, including loss of loved ones, job changes, and new relationships. I also thought about the many transitions and changes that I had experienced. I was reminded that following Christ and his will for my life is a journey with a wide variety of experiences and changes.

Carol concluded with a soothing collection of Christian music and pictures of nature, along with poetry and Scripture. Her final quote was from Jeremiah 29:11 (see above). I enjoyed the presentation, but not until later did I realize how much my soul had been fed and encouraged. I was reminded that God is in control: no matter what we face, we do not need to be afraid.

Our board continued to wrestle with how the current uncertain times provide new opportunities to serve the needs of our members and congregations. The board was led to direct management toward finding new ways to equip people for facing economic challenges that arise and for responding with generosity when those challenges affect others.

Even while leaders of God's people were living in exile and dealing with painful memories of defeat and deportation, the Lord's word came to them through the prophet: "Build houses and live in them; plant gardens and eat what they produce. . . . For surely I know the plans I have for you, says the LORD, plans for your welfare and not for harm, to give you a future with hope" (Jer 29:5, 11).

—Larry D. Miller of Goshen, Indiana, is president and CEO of Everence, a financial and mutual aid organization.

God Chose Us

> You who bring good tidings to Zion, go up on a high
>   mountain.
> You who bring good tidings to Jerusalem, lift up your voice
>   with a shout,
> lift it up, do not be afraid; say to the towns of Judah,
>   "Here is your God!"
>
> —Isaiah 40:9 NIV

Carolyn was sleeping peacefully, so I tried not to awaken her as I slowly unzipped the front door of our little tent and crawled out into the cold night air. Over to the west, just beyond the Snake River, the dark silhouette of the Teton Mountain range rose jagged into the sky. In the darkness I could just make out the big clumps of sagebrush. Crickets were chirping loudly, and an owl hooted down by the creek. I stood awkwardly to my feet, trying not to stumble over anything.

Then I looked up. What I saw literally staggered me; I could barely keep my balance as I swept my eyes across the most brilliant display of stars I had ever seen! The cold Wyoming night air was as clear as outer space, and every tiny part of the sky was sparkling. Suddenly I felt such a profound sense of awe that my legs became weak. As I struggled to keep my balance, I was filled with wonder. "O God! What are we pitiful little human beings that you are even aware of us?"

I thought of an experiment done when the Hubble Space Telescope was still new in its orbit. Hour after hour the scientists had aimed it at a tiny point in one of the darkest sections of the sky, so focused that its field of vision was equivalent to that of a grain of sand held at arm's length. Even in that tiny, dark patch of sky, the time exposure revealed dozens of galaxies far away, each of them containing billions of stars!

Within the range of the Hubble Telescope are somewhere close to 100 billion such galaxies. In turn, a typical galaxy such as our own Milky Way contains about 100 billion stars. Ten thousand billion billion stars! Ten sextillion stars!

Working with Habitat for Humanity, the Fuller Center for Housing, and other organizations, I have made dozens of trips into some of the most troubled parts of this planet. Even more demanding at times have been some of the scores of board meetings I have survived over the years. Often I have been struck by the similarities between international battlefields and the conflicts in the boardrooms. People get hurt in both. Anger and domination replace empathy and harmony. The grand visions that may have inspired the founding of nations or of NGOs (nongovernmental organizations) are often lost in battle.

And yet, for some inscrutable reason far beyond my poor grasp, God has chosen to work through us frustrating, fallible human beings. And sometimes, miracle of miracles, great and beautiful works are accomplished through even us!

I believe the kind of leadership called for in the boardroom is a combination of personal humility and the audacity to believe that God does indeed want to do something great through our efforts. When I come home from another difficult board meeting or a trip to another place of international conflict, I'm sometimes asked where I find my hope. Then I think back to that starry sky over the Rockies.

I think of the One who created all of that splendor as well as my beloved wife, asleep in that little tent, and the crickets chirping in the sagebrush around us. "There," I answer, "is the One who fills me with hope. No, with more than just hope—with absolute assurance: 'Our God is here. Let's get on with the agenda!'"

—Don Mosley lives at Jubilee Partners, a Christian community of which he was one of the founders in Gomer, Georgia. He is author of *Faith Beyond Borders: Doing Justice in a Dangerous World.*

Holding to the Standards of Justice, Mercy, and Humility

> He has showed you, O mortal, what is good.
> And what does the LORD require of you?
> To act justly and to love mercy
> and to walk humbly with your God.
>
> —Micah 6:8 NIV

When I visited Port-au-Prince, Haiti, days after the January 12, 2010, earthquake, I saw total devastation. Piles of concrete were everywhere; on the hillsides, sheets and quilts and scraps were pulled together to provide some means of shelter for the victims of this horrendous disaster. Upon my return to Georgia, I was convinced that Habitat for Humanity had to make a bold response.

The challenge, however, was that the immediate response was calling for something that was inconsistent with our traditional methods. Habitat for Humanity focuses on helping families obtain permanent housing. The immediate need in Haiti, however, was for emergency shelter—a temporary housing solution. Another Habitat for Humanity hallmark is not to give houses away. Homeowners are required to contribute to their housing solutions: they pay off a nonprofit mortgage on their homes. That was out of the question for the more than 1.2 million people in Haiti made homeless by the devastating earthquake. What were we to do?

As I often do, I turned to what I have come to call my "life verse," Micah 6:8. My grandmother, a civil-rights and human-rights pioneer as well as New Jersey Congresswoman Millicent Fenwick, used to recite this verse (see above) to me every time I saw her. I have come to rely heavily on its message.

The three themes of the passage—justice, mercy, and humility—give us clear and simple direction for how we are to live and what we are to do. First, Micah tells us to act justly and to love mercy—actions that are at the heart of Habitat for Humanity's ministry. Mercy requires action, and we offer compassionate response to those who lack adequate shelter.

We also see our role as helping to create a more-just world. We believe that everyone should have the opportunity to live in a decent, affordable house. That means that we do whatever we can to mold our world into God's image and to bring hope to people who are suffering. Seeking justice means focusing daily on a way of life that is directed by God's unconditional and immeasurable love.

The just and merciful action concerning Haiti was to create and distribute emergency shelter kits while also making plans toward developing permanent housing solutions.

But justice and compassion are not just about our outward activities. Micah is telling us that we must pay attention to the way we treat one another within the organization.

And wrapped in all of that is a right relationship with God. We cannot forget to offer ourselves humbly before God and to examine whether our agenda is God's agenda. When we make decisions—monumental and mundane—we must ask if we truly want to know and do God's will; then we must seek God's wisdom through prayer and study of Scripture. Our Habitat for Humanity board has recently made the commitment to be more focused on the biblical principles that guide our work.

If we build our lives on the Micah verses, we will be guided by these three standards: justice, mercy, and humility before God.

—Jonathan T. M. Reckford of Atlanta, Georgia, is president and CEO of Habitat for Humanity International.

Beyond the Valley of the Now

> After the death of Moses the servant of the LORD, the
> LORD said to Joshua son of Nun, Moses' aide: "Moses my
> servant is dead. Now then, you and all these people, get
> ready to cross the Jordan River into the land I am about to
> give to them—to the Israelites. I will give you every place
> where you set your foot, as I promised Moses . . . As I was
> with Moses, so I will be with you; I will never leave you nor
> forsake you."
>
> —Joshua 1:1-5 NIV

Nothing is more certain, we are told, than death and taxes. We'll add one more certainty: change. Life is a constant pulse of change, at both the macrolevel and the microlevel. On the organizational level, the change of leaders often marks the ending or the beginning of an era. Leadership matters. Leaders make a difference in every organization.

In the journey of the Hebrew people, Moses served well the purposes of God, leading them out of Egypt and through the wilderness, to the Promised Land. But alas, his term of service was complete without the full realization of the goal. The time had come for someone else to step up and serve the community as leader. And in what appears to have been a seamless continuation of the original purposes of God, the leadership transfer from Moses to Joshua takes place like the turning of the page from Deuteronomy to the book of Joshua. In this transition, we read God's words of assurance and promise: "I will be with you as I was with Moses. I will not fail you or abandon you" (NLT).

Signs throughout the tenure of Moses' leadership indicated that God was with him. God was guiding them in the whole exodus story: crossing the Red Sea, manna from heaven and water from a rock, pillar of cloud by day and pillar of fire by night. And the Ten Commandments guided their behavior. God's promise to be with the new leader as with the former leader was a comfort to Joshua and the whole community.

The most important decision a governing board makes is the selection of a director. Leadership transitions can make or break an organization. In the text printed above, the leadership change from Moses to Joshua is clear and unambiguous. In our organizations, however, transition is not always as clear-cut, nor is the reason for the change. And yet change is inevitable as an organization matures. God continues to move and work out God's divine purposes through organizations.

As our board navigates its way through a leadership transition, consider the ways that God has been with our organization. What are the markings of God's faithfulness? Let's name them and celebrate them! As we anticipate moving into the new chapter, let's approach it as a new day, with the certainty of God's faithfulness and blessing. May this thought be the source of our hope and our strength as we journey beyond the valley of the now into the land of the not yet.

May the word of God to Joshua also be a word of encouragement for us, both as individuals and collectively as a board: "Have I not commanded you? Be strong and courageous. Do not be afraid; do not be discouraged, for the LORD your God will be with you wherever you go" (Josh 1:9).

—Terry Shue of Kidron, Ohio, is director of leadership development for Mennonite Church USA.

Following the Servant Jesus in Volatile Times

> When [Jesus] had finished washing their feet, he put on his
> clothes and returned to his place. "Do you understand what
> I have done for you?" he asked them. "You call me 'Teacher'
> and 'Lord,' and rightly so, for that is what I am. Now that
> I, your Lord and Teacher, have washed your feet, you also
> should wash one another's feet. I have set you an example
> that you should do as I have done for you. Very truly I tell
> you, no servant is greater than his master, nor is a messen-
> ger greater than the one who sent him. Now that you know
> these things, you will be blessed if you do them."
>
> —John 13:12-17 NIV

Don't break out the party hats yet! When a global recession nears
an end, new ones are in the making. This is likely to be a volatile
decade. As a consequence, we as Christian leaders need to reimagine how to live our lives and run our organizations as we follow
the servant Jesus.

In all seasons, Jesus calls us to seek first the kingdom. We
race into a new decade where growing numbers of our neighbors locally and globally will be hammered by waves of change.
As a consequence, we all need to reimagine how to steward our
personal lives. First, we need to reduce our own economic vulnerability to increase the availability of our time and resources
to serve the needy. We begin by asking, "How much is enough?"
How much do we need to spend for our housing, transportation, wardrobe, vacations, and entertainment? In times like this,
faithfulness requires that we all model and help those we work
with to discover how to create new forms of whole-life stewardship that is both simpler and more celebrative.

During the 2008–10 recession, many people in poor communities instinctively reached out and helped one another. In mid-
dle-class communities, however, those who lost jobs and homes
felt isolated and lonely in the suburbs. A suburban Presbyterian
Church created a midweek soup supper where people could come
to hear each other's stories and offer mutual support. In uncertain times, servanthood needs to include creating mutual-care

networks in both our congregations and our Christian organizations. These networks also need to create new ways to reach out to neighbors near and far.

Jesus models a kind of servant leadership in which he washes feet, hugs kids, and hangs out with the wrong kind of people. Following Jesus involves being servants to all who are within our organizations, taking on menial chores, and looking for ways to care. It also involves spending time in discovering what God has to teach us. Leadership means learning to anticipate new challenges. In these uncertain times, leaders must learn to identify new opportunities.

We also need to learn that servanthood means learning to listen to what God is saying through all the disparate voices in our churches or Christian organizations. I have had the opportunity to work with twenty- and thirty-year-olds who are creating new expressions of church, community, and urban mission. Instead of top-down leadership models, these young people work as teams, trying to listen to what God is saying. As Christine Sine leads Mustard Seed Associates, she uses the Quaker discernment process to listen to one another. We not only hear one another's ideas; we also hear how God is at work in each other's lives. We catch an emerging sense of what God seems to be stirring up in our organizations.

It is particularly essential that we listen to and invite the ideas and imagination of the young in our churches and Christian organizations. Their input and innovative ideas are rarely invited. Youth are often more in touch with the changing times. God is helping them imagine whole new ways to express the good news of Christ in their lives, worship, and especially in responding to the needs of others.

At the core the call to follow Jesus in all seasons is the call to set aside our own ideas, needs, and insecurities and learn to listen, especially to the poor and the young. In these turbulent times, those of us in leadership need to pay much more careful attention to the new dreams and ideas that God is stirring up in the lives of others, telling us how to be faithful servants of Christ.

—Tom Sine of Seattle, Washington, is the author of numerous books, including *The New Conspirators*. He is a founding member of the Mustard Seed Associates.

In Change There Is Opportunity

> The LORD spoke to Joshua son of Nun, Moses' assistant, say-
> ing, "My servant Moses is dead. Now proceed to cross the
> Jordan, you and all this people, into the land that I am giv-
> ing to them, to the Israelites. . . . I will not fail you or forsake
> you; . . . for the LORD your God is with you wherever you go."
> —Joshua 1:1-2, 5, 9

For forty years Millard Fuller pursued his vision of eliminating
poverty housing. First at Koinonia Farm, then through Habitat
for Humanity International, and finally with The Fuller Center
for Housing—Millard's faith, exceptional promotional skills, and
sheer force built a modest house that 300 thousand families could
call home.

Millard died unexpectedly on February 3, 2009. His last ministry, The Fuller Center for Housing, was not quite four years old.
Drawing on more than thirty years of experience, it had rapidly
grown to have covenant partners in fifty U.S. cities and fourteen
countries. On the afternoon we buried Millard, a group of board
members met at his residence to strategize. We were confronted
by a host of serious issues. Could this young ministry continue
without Millard? How would we turn a personality-driven ministry into one driven by mission? What were we called to do?

We prayed. We tried to listen closely for the "still small voice"
(1 Kings 19:12 KJV). Millard often said that we were about the
Lord's work, not his. We had, in our short four-year history, begun
to instill hope in communities around the world. We had obliga-
tions to meet and hopes to fulfill.

We knew we couldn't replace Millard: those with his unique
skills and profound faith are few. Our thoughts turned to Moses:
after forty years of leading his people through the wilderness
and teaching them God's will, he was denied entry to the Promised Land. Like the children of Israel, we asked, "How do we go
on? Who will replace our leader?"

The Lord had a plan. The exodus was more than one man's
vision: it was a divinely ordained mission. Joshua was called to lead
the people into the Promised Land. God told him, "My servant

Moses is dead. Now proceed to cross the Jordan, you and all this people. . . . As I was with Moses, so I will be with you. I will not fail you or forsake you. . . . Be strong and courageous; do not be frightened or dismayed, for the LORD your God is with you wherever you go" (Josh 1:2, 5, 9).

God refocused our attention from the fallen leader to the mission. God told us to move on without fear and promised to be with us. Our young board committed to do the same. We had a common commitment to the ministry and a shared understanding of our foundational principles. We agreed that in change there is opportunity. We reminded ourselves that the future requires us to be adaptive and patient.

Executive transitions, especially those involving a founder, present a real challenge. A successful transition requires a solid board, a clear and mutually accepted understanding of the mission, and a bold measure of faith. Seeking, listening for, and accepting the Lord's guidance are essential, but acting on that guidance falls to those who are left behind.

The Lord has blessed the Fuller Center through our transition, and God continues to smile on the work that Millard started. But it is no longer one man's vision: instead, it is a vision that is being shared and made real by thousands of supporters and volunteers around the world.

—David Snell of Americus, Georgia, is president and CEO of The Fuller Center for Housing, an ecumenical Christian ministry dedicated to making decent shelter a reality for all of God's people in need.

Faith Stories Build Community

> May God be gracious to us and bless us and make his face
>   to shine upon us, [Selah]
> that your way may be known upon earth, your saving power
>   among all nations.
> Let the peoples praise you, O God; let all the peoples praise you.
> Let the nations be glad and sing for joy,
>   for you judge the peoples with equity and guide the
>   nations upon earth. [Selah]
> Let the peoples praise you, O God; let all the peoples praise you.
> The earth has yielded its increase; God, our God, has blessed us.
> May God continue to bless us; let all the ends of the earth
>   revere him.
>
> —Psalm 67

In 2008 I was invited to assist the governing board of an area conference to implement its governance system and facilitate a process of envisioning the future. The conference included rural, predominately white congregations as well as urban multiracial congregations. The governing board reflected the diversity of member congregations, including Hispanic, African American, Ethiopian, and Caucasian board members.

As I observed this diverse body at work, I was impressed by their dedication to the church and the depth of their faith commitment. But effective communication seemed difficult. During a previous meeting, a disagreement emerged over expenditures related to a capital campaign. It led to an argument and misunderstandings, threatening to weaken mutual trust. While the meeting concluded with an agreement, I questioned if this group was in a position to focus clearly on their major task of envisioning the future.

At the next meeting some weeks later, the board chair read from Psalm 67 and invited board members to share what the Scripture meant to them. I was in awe as I heard story after story about members' faith journeys and their connection to the present. Several stories told how they were first exposed to the Christian faith, how they became connected to Mennonites, what their faith means to them now, and their extreme gratitude for the role of the conference in their present assignment. I heard these themes, based on Psalm 67:

- God's generous blessings on us
- Making God's way known
- God's saving power
- Judging people with equity

To my amazement, the board assignment to envision the future became a continuation of this storytelling process. Board members, having done their homework, were eager to express what they believed God desired for their future. They were eager to learn from each other as they shared differing perspectives. Throughout the meeting, I heard repeated laughter as people were connecting with each other in a joyous mood. Group wisdom emerged as members yielded to each other in search of their future mission.

In reflecting on this special day, I am impressed with the power of story in building community. Our faith is a journey that can be told by story. Board members each have a story, a faith journey. So do the organizations they govern. I've come to believe that when we're aware of the presence of God in our own personal story, we're more likely to notice how God is at work in the organizations we govern. Sharing faith stories in the boardroom builds community.

—Karl C. Sommers of Goshen, Indiana, is a governance and leadership coach.

Treasure in Clay Jars

> For we do not proclaim ourselves; we proclaim Jesus Christ
> as Lord and ourselves as your slaves for Jesus' sake. For it is
> the God who said, "Let light shine out of darkness," who
> has shone in our hearts to give the light of the knowledge
> of the glory of God in the face of Jesus Christ. But we have
> this treasure in clay jars, so that it may be made clear that
> this extraordinary power belongs to God and does not
> come from us.
> —Paul, in 2 Corinthians 4:5-7

I had the privilege of participating in the first meeting of the governing board of Mennonite Church USA, the integration of two Mennonite groups. The board needed to deal with significant, urgent issues:

- By what principles will we govern?
- What are the desired values and outcomes for this new church?
- What action is needed for an insolvent publishing agency?

The board chair emphasized the importance of operating from a spiritual center. He suggested that the board integrate worship as an essential part of their work. Having helped to plan this meeting, and knowing the heavy agenda that faced us, the skeptic in me questioned, "Will the real business of the board get done?" The first meeting had been postponed due to a national emergency, making this meeting even more urgent.

A board member used the Scripture quoted above in his opening meditation. He suggested that the "treasure in clay jars" was a metaphor to emphasize the awesome trust that God bestows on us as ordinary people with the good news of Jesus Christ (the treasure). It is being carried around by us humans (clay jars), with all of our weaknesses and faults.

Our leader warned that "carrying the treasure forward will not be a lighthearted waltz through the meadow. In the words of Paul, it will require endurance, perseverance, persistence, patience, and humility."

As the board worked through its agenda, it stopped at strategic points to pray for God's direction. At times they paused to sing, "Gentle Shepherd, come and lead us, for we need you to help us find our way."[7]

A special spiritual moment occurred when local church planters joined the meeting. They distributed strips of cloth and invited everyone to take them to a container of water, whereupon they praised God together and offered special prayer for this new work. The strips were later sewed into a towel to be used for baptisms in their new congregation.

I was struck with how the meeting's flow integrated storytelling, Scripture, song, and prayer around the core business issues that needed to be resolved. And yes, the meeting objectives were achieved in spite of (because of?) what seemed like detours along the way.

This meeting reaffirmed my belief that boards of faith-based organizations do their best work when they intentionally operate as discerning leadership boards. This means that the board's first priority is to take the treasure in clay jars and discern the God questions: (1) What is God doing now in our organization? (2) What is God's desired future for our organization? Only after the board answers these questions is it ready to address its regular agenda.

—Karl C. Sommers of Goshen, Indiana, is a governance and leadership coach.

Scaling Mountains

> Enlarge the site of your tent, and let the curtains of your
>   habitation be stretched out;
> do not hold back; lengthen your cords and strengthen
>   your stakes.
> —Isaiah 54:2

> Put me to the test, says the LORD of hosts;
> see if I will not . . . pour down for you an overflowing blessing.
> —Malachi 3:10

> Now to [God,] who by the power at work within us
> is able to accomplish abundantly far more than all we can
>   ask or imagine,
> to him be glory in the church and in Christ Jesus to all
>   generations, for ever and ever. Amen.
> —Paul, in Ephesians 3:20-21

I was the only American on a team of Indians, most of them doctors. Our assignment was to evaluate a medical program that had peaked and was now seeking to invent a new future for itself. Its daunting goal was to rid South India of the scourge of leprosy. The days were long, the nights unbearably hot, and the way ahead unclear.

"Why," I asked myself in a hot night of sleeplessness, "should I, only months from my eightieth birthday, be preoccupied with a disease that has burdened humanity since before Bible times? Shouldn't I rather be at home with my wife, who is in the early stages of Parkinson's disease? Surely it would be more enjoyable to be in my fully equipped but mostly idle woodworking shop."

As these thoughts coursed through my tired mind, I reminded myself that I was on the South India plain, with an occasional outcropping of rock, worn smooth by centuries of rain and wind; yet on Indian's northern border is the awe-inspiring snow-covered Himalayan Mountain range. It was not until 1953 that a brave and determined Sir Edmund Hillary became the first human to scale Mount Everest, its highest peak. When asked why he was willing to risk life and limb for this treacherous and arduous undertaking, his simple answer was "Because it is there."

So it is that in the course of a lifetime, people and organizations face daunting challenges. It is saddening to consider how many hypothetical Everests never are climbed, how many promising expeditions stall in the foothills.

Hillary, we remember, did not make his historic climb on a whim. He studied the mountainous terrain carefully. He availed himself of the best equipment available. He chose the most propitious time for his expedition. But he did not allow that formidable mountain to intimidate him. He assaulted it with a steely determination and confidence bigger than the mountain.

Leaders, someone has observed, are either risk-takers, caretakers, or undertakers. New ventures are always accompanied by risk. Directors unwilling to risk for a worthy cause run the far greater risk of creeping irrelevance and slow death.

To risk does not mean to ignore caution. Risking, like most everything else, must be learned. Many boards are so adverse to change that they resist it too long; when it is forced on them, it is jolting and unnecessarily risky. Great boards learn to go with the flow. They read the signs of the times and change incrementally as the early signs of the need for it begin to appear.

Great boards allow innovation to prove its merit on the margins. After they have perfected it, they apply it on a grander scale and thus keep the organization on the cutting edge. In the passage quoted above, the apostle Paul reminds us that God's power is available to us to "accomplish abundantly far more than all we can ask or imagine. To him be glory in the church and in Christ Jesus to all generations, forever and ever. Amen."

—Edgar Stoesz of Akron, Pennsylvania, has worked for Mennonite Central Committee and served on many nonprofit boards, including chairing Habitat for Humanity International. He is author of numerous books, including *Doing Good Even Better*.

Risking for Success

> Then [Jesus] told this parable: A man had a fig tree planted
> in his vineyard; and he came looking for fruit on it and
> found none. So he said to the gardener, "See here! For
> three years I have come looking for fruit on this fig tree, and
> still I find none. Cut it down! Why should it be wasting the
> soil?" He replied, "Sir, let it alone for one more year, until
> I dig around it and put manure on it. If it bears fruit next
> year, well and good; but if not, you can cut it down."
>
> —Luke 13:6-9

Most projects start with a burst of enthusiasm. This new innovation, it is believed, will usher in the kingdom of God. Then a time
of grace follows while the idea is given an opportunity to demonstrate its merit. Eventually—sometimes sooner, sometimes later—a
moment of truth arrives. Does it deserve our confidence, or was it a
boondoggle from the outset?

In studying corporate projects, the Harvard professor Rosabeth
Moss Kanter has observed that generally "there came a point when
the leaders started to lose faith in a project. They were exhausted
and recognized that 'this is harder than we thought.'" It led her to
what is sometimes called Kanter's Law: "Every undertaking looks
like a failure in the middle."

Thomas Edison, who travailed through innumerable failures
before giving us the incandescent light bulb, said, "Many of life's
failures are people who did not realize how close they were to success when they gave up." The most difficult decision an airplane
captain has to make when a mechanical problem appears midway
on a transoceanic flight is whether to return to the place of origin
or risk making the destination.

Winston Churchill, who doggedly refused to surrender to relent-
less German bombing, divulged his secret in a memorable if unorthodox speech. After surveying his audience, he intoned: "Never [*pause*],
never [*pause*], never give up." He took his seat. Speech over. Point
made, by a man qualified by experience to make it.

Sometimes leaders refuse to recognize that a project is failing
because of a claustrophobic fear of failure. They fear losing face,

admitting wrong! In so doing, they deny themselves the wisdom that can come from failure and thus continue an activity that can at best only half succeed. They settle for mediocrity instead of risking for success.

In his efforts that resulted in the Green Revolution and feeding millions, Norman Borlaug came upon two plant geneticists disputing which strain of wheat was superior. After hearing them, Borlaug responded, "I'm interested only in a strain whose superiority is so evident that it can be recognized while riding by on a bicycle." Borlaug refused to settle for good: he insisted on the best!

When do we call in the bulldozer to root out a nonproductive tree? When do we, as in this parable, plead for another year? That is the most excruciating decision that directors are called upon to make. When does persistence become stubborn folly?

In arriving at such a critical decision, directors should gather all the available facts and analyze them objectively. Often the facts speak for themselves. Sometimes they lead to new and unintended alternatives. This is when directors call on their experience, wisdom, and spiritual intuition to do what they consider to be right. "Success is not permanent," said Winston Churchill, "and failure need not be fatal; it is the courage to continue that counts."

—Edgar Stoesz of Akron, Pennsylvania, has worked for Mennonite Central Committee and served on many nonprofit boards, including chairing Habitat For Humanity International. He is author of numerous books, including *Doing Good Even Better*.

Whom Shall I Fear?

> God is our refuge and strength, a very present help in trouble.
> Therefore we will not fear, though the earth should change,
>   though the mountains shake in the heart of the sea;
> though its waters roar and foam,
>   though the mountains tremble with its tumult.
>   —Psalm 46:1-3

As South Dakota farmers, our favorite time of the year is the harvest season. To see one wagon after another leave the field, loaded with the bounty of God's earth, the fruit of our labors, is deeply satisfying. But with it also comes a subtle sadness. As the mammoth combine circles the field, the wildlife habitat shrinks. Frightened pheasants, raccoons, rabbits, mice, fox, and deer reluctantly dart from their lairs to seek a new refuge. With wide eyes and skittish flight patterns, they return to the last vestiges of remaining rows. They are, in one word, frantic.

Rabbits are usually the first to venture out—running in circles, only to return to their starting point. Mice are keenly aware of the circling hawks, poised in a menacing pattern, ready to make the nosedive that guarantees their evening meal. As the combine swallows the last rows of corn, all the animals scatter to take refuge in the fencerows. We wonder how they will fare in their new surroundings.

Fear is also a human phenomenon, and the boardroom is not exempt. Fear has many layers of complexity. Physiologically, our blood pressure rises, our pulse and breathing rates increase, the endocrine system releases numerous chemicals within our body—all to help us address this fear. Emotionally we feel vulnerable and are prone to resentment, rage, and revenge. We seek whatever means necessary for survival.

How quickly we forget, "The LORD is my light and my salvation; whom shall I fear?" (Ps 27:1). Whether we function as individuals or in board teams, fear needs to be controlled. It can motivate, inspire, and encourage us out of our complacency. Fear can also paralyze us; yet God, we remind ourselves, is not afraid.

When gathered as a board, we are functioning in a leadership role. Each person is part of the team and has something to contribute. Each is, however, wired differently. We represent diverse passions and concerns, but we are committed to the process of working together to discern where God is working so that we can participate. We seek God's Spirit to help us recognize the "good of the whole" and to find strategies to get there.

At times in the life of all organizations, we individually and corporately as a board feel like the terrified rabbits that are rapidly losing their shelter. Our organization is shifting beneath us, and we are fearful. It's natural to feel fear when under threat. But it helps to name our fears, not to run from them. Philip Yancey reminds us that "fear opens us to God's leading." When we are vulnerable, we're more ready to listen to God's Spirit and more able to participate in God's work in progress.

With our hope in the God of the Psalms, and with prayerful courage, may we address our fears and move ahead with audacity, seeking God's will for our organization.

—Sharon and Anne Waltner live in Freeman, South Dakota. Sharon served as moderator of Mennonite Church USA in 2007–9 and is a healthcare facilities leadership consultant. Daughter Anne completed a doctorate of musical arts degree and contemplates farming as a vocation.

How Does a Christian Organization Plan?

Trust in the Lord with all your heart, and do not rely on
your own insight.
In all your ways acknowledge him, and he will make
straight your paths.

—Proverbs 3:5-6

"Aim at nothing," the statement goes, "and you will hit it every time." True! Planning is taking aim. It is an essential board function. So, how does a Christian organization plan? How is God involved in planning? What do the Scriptures have to say about planning? Leaders of Christian organizations should ponder these question seriously.

Proverbs 29:18 tells us that "where there is no vision, the people perish" (KJV). God has called us as leaders to envision a future for our organizations that will be pleasing to God. Does your ministry have a vision that can help drive a strategic plan?

A plan is as likely to take God out of the plan as it is to put God into the plan. In James (4:13-15), we read: "Now listen, you who say, 'Today or tomorrow we will go to this or that city, spend a year there, carry on business and make money.' Why, you do not even know what will happen tomorrow. What is your life? You are a mist that appears for a little while and then vanishes. Instead, you ought to say, 'If it is the Lord's will, we will live and do this or that'" (NIV).

All plans should be made with a sense of humility and the recognition that ultimately God governs the affairs of all institutions, including the one you are helping to lead. Have you prayed about this process, to make sure that God has not been left out?

A plan that is too small dishonors God and leaves people uninspired. The great evangelist Dwight L. Moody declared, "We honor God when we ask for great things. It is humiliating to think that we are satisfied with small results." Are your plans simply a continuation of what you have been doing for years? Is lack of money or people causing you to think too small?

A plan that is unrealistically big also dishonors God and leaves people discouraged. The Tower of Babel was going to reach to the heavens. God was not pleased and caused the people to become confused and abandon the project unfinished. Does your plan over-reach to such an extent that no one believes it to be achievable?

Ministry planning is an inherently mystical, complicated, and integrated process. The value of a plan is often difficult to assess by looking at its isolated components. Robert Louis Stevenson advised, "Don't judge each day by the harvest you reap, but by the seeds you plant."

Planning is more successful when numerous wise people are involved. Proverbs 15:22 tells us that plans fail for lack of counsel, but "with many advisers," they are more successful. How many stakeholders are involved in your planning process (employees, volunteers, donors, outsiders)?

Many plans falter because of poor execution. Jesus, who was in perfect union with God, had followers who did not want to follow the plan; they wanted to go in a different direction. Are we spending as much time thinking about the execution of our plan as we are about the plan itself?

Although leading a board to envision the future is hard work, we remember that we are not alone. Ultimately the vineyard belongs to God, and we are God's workers.

—David Williams of Phoenix, Arizona, is president and CEO of the Make-A-Wish Foundation of America. He previously served as executive vice president and COO of Habitat for Humanity International.

Discerning the Future and the Calling

> Keep this Book of the Law always on your lips; meditate on
> it day and night, so that you may be careful to do everything
> written in it. Then you will be prosperous and successful.
>
> —Joshua 1:8 NIV

This Scripture comes on the heels of Moses' death as the people prepare to move into the Promised Land. What a mix of emotions must have been present: uncertainty, fear, anticipation, anxiety, and frustration. It was all there! As stewards of organizations, few have faced such an overwhelming transition as the people of Israel after wandering homeless forty years in the wilderness. And to what were they called in that situation? To meditate on God's way unceasingly!

Meditation allows for holy connection time. It allows for boundary time, for space between "what is" and "what is to come." It taps into our highest relationship, the source of all and ultimately the Knower of all that is best for us and our organization. Meditation is what a wise friend has called, "Letting the prunes soak."

When we face major challenges, our tendency is to do the opposite. We often feel determined to act boldly and quickly. Something needs attention, something needs doing, we want to take control. Decisions feel good, but we often confuse action with results. In times like this, we should remember that the greater the challenge, the more discernment is required to move away from our egos and self-identities and instead seek a guidance that knows better than us!

We access great power in allowing for this connecting and discernment time during board meetings. I remember the mistake I made as chair of a national church board. A contentious subject appeared on the agenda, requiring a major decision. The recess hour was approaching, and I pushed the meeting to action.

That evening I was approached by several members who expressed a concern that the process felt controlled, with inadequate time for discussion and discernment. After a restless night, I suggested that the action be reopened for discussion, but first we would take time to pray and discern together.

Our action the previous day was affirmed, but in a totally different atmosphere of trust and agreement. In short, it was touched by the Spirit! It was a valuable lesson. When boards have tough decisions, or when their organization's direction and calling are unclear, nothing is more important than heeding the prophet's words to meditate on it day and night before going forward!

Following tough decisions, it is equally important to celebrate that we stayed the course: we acted with integrity, continued to move along, and remained faithful to God and ourselves. Then we hear again the wonderful promise of Joshua: "Be strong and courageous; do not be frightened or dismayed, for the LORD your God is with you wherever you go."

—David M. Wine of Overland Park, Kansas, is president and CEO of MAX Insurance Companies, North America. He was moderator of the Church of the Brethren in 1996–97.

Prayers

God who led the Israelites with a pillar of cloud by day
> and a pillar of fire by night,
we come seeking your guidance for [*name the issue at hand*].

Our path is not clear.
Our vision is limited.
We cannot see where our decision will take us.

Yet we know you care about even the smallest matters of our lives:
> you knew us in our mother's womb,
> the hairs of our head are numbered,
> and you promise to go with us even into dark valleys.

And so we pause to rest in you,
> to release our uncertainty and fear,
> to trust in your good purposes,
> to open ourselves to your Spirit's prompting,
> and to wait for your light to shine on our path.

[*Pause for 2–3 minutes of silence, allowing people to become aware of their fears or concerns and to release them into God's care.*]

Lead us in your light, O God;
> show us your paths of truth and righteousness,
> grant us courage to follow you,
> and bless our decision that it may bring healing, peace, and
>> joy in the world.

We pray in the name of Christ, who is the Light of the World. Amen.

—Marlene Kropf is associate professor of spiritual formation and worship, Associated Mennonite Biblical Seminary, and the former denominational minister of worship for Mennonite Church USA.

Holy God, by your Spirit many people have traveled far and wide, over unchartered territory, into unknown places. You led with fire and with cloud. You spoke to leaders. You engraved commandments. You never left your people stranded.

We call on your name, Holy Guide, to mark our path with unmistakable signs today. We face major decisions, and our journey seems complicated. Options, choices, possibilities are ahead for this board. [*Pause to name decisions.*]

Grant us clarity and conviction. Give us courage and commitment. Bind us together so that this path will be ours to walk together.

Holy God, we trust your Spirit to accompany us and to empower us for this time and this decision. Amen.

—Dorothy Nickel Friesen has spent her professional career in the English classroom as teacher and the last twenty-eight years as a Mennonite pastor, seminary administrator, and conference minister.

Holy God, entrust us with the wisdom of Solomon as we prepare to make our decisions. Grant to us wisdom and discernment to know the right path and the good decision. And give us such clarity that we move forward with the boldness of faith. Amen.

—David Johnson Rowe is copastor of Greenfield Hill Congregational Church, Fairfield, Connecticut.

8

Meditations When Conflict Threatens Board Unity

Introduction

Governing boards are not immune to conflict and disunity. They are actually more effective when they are able to handle strong differences of opinion or dissent. Great boards are not known by the absence of disagreement. They are known by what they disagree over and by how they handle the disagreement. Unresolved and poorly managed conflict can lead to disunity. Disunity can be devastating to an organization.

Many faith-based nonprofit boards put a high premium on getting along. They think (mistakenly) that debate is tension producing and therefore unwelcome. We know CEOs (and chairs!) who go to great lengths to keep from having their recommendations subjected to open discussion. We also know many directors who are too timid to enter into the path of a heated debate. Although this attitude may produce orderly meetings, it underestimates the value of collective discernment. It may also suggest that a few are trying to hypermanage the board agenda and in the process denying themselves the wisdom that comes with an open search for the best solution. Be thankful when good and lively discussion ensues, even if at points it tips into tension. It means that the hearts and minds of the members are engaged.

Great nonprofit boards bring into the governance process individuals with different perspectives. These leaders think independently but come to agreement and in the end speak with one voice. They use a structured approach in dealing with strategic issues, opportunities, or even executive recommendations. Good leaders recognize that many possible pathways offer the potential for upside gain as well as downstream risk. Great chairs facilitate genuine board engagement by inviting input on a given subject from all the members, airing both the advantages and disadvantages. Such leadership legitimates independent opinion. Some boards are even experimenting with use of a "dissent agenda," a way of placing on the agenda some issues or matters about which the chair and CEO know there will be disagreement. The technique serves to generate creative alternative points of view but perhaps more profoundly to legitimate the value of differences of perspective.

Nevertheless, differences of opinion, if poorly handled, can lead to conflict. At its best, board work is a collaborative, deliberative process. It can, however, also be the setting for clashing egos. Unrestrained ego is the enemy of good board work. It does not ask what course of action will serve the cause best. Ego-trippers want their own way all the time, regardless of cost. Their ego sees only what it wants to see to get its way. Everything else is seen as the enemy, to be put down. Its highest objective is to prevail, whether right or not. The unrestrained ego frustrates good decision making and makes disagreements into conflicts. Such an ego has no place in the boardroom. In an ego-dominated atmosphere, servanthood has been trumped by personal ambition and arrogance. Boards facing this sad dynamic do well to put their routine agenda aside and seek to restore a healthy spiritual center. Two helpful books are *The Little Book of Conflict Transformation*, by John Paul Lederach, and *A New Earth*, by Eckhart Tolle (esp. chap. 3).[1]

Disagreement need not result in conflict. It should not be seen as disunity. At its base, disagreement is just another way of seeing things. The role of the board is to decide which point of view will prevail. The unfortunate fact is that many boards are so afraid of disagreement that they let the difference fester until it becomes a protracted conflict.

Roberts' Rules of Order are the recognized authority on how meetings are to be conducted. Although these rules provide "order," they may not provide enough space or time for the entire board to come to a common mind. Other boards use a more informal process of decision making. Quakers use periods of silence and wait for consensus. Regardless of the practice used, it is important that there be opportunity for the free exchange of perspectives, and that once a decision is made, the board stands in solidarity.

Select a meditation from this chapter that best speaks to the situation facing you. It may be beneficial to page through other chapters, particularly chapter 10, since themes in these chapters overlap. Be free to insert your thoughts and adapt to your circumstances. Conclude your devotional time with one of the prayers printed below, again feeling free to add to it and adapt it. Some may want to repeat the Lord's Prayer in unison or sing a song together. Use silence and thoughtful pauses. Be relaxed and worshipful. Make it your goal to set a spiritual tone that will pervade the entire meeting.

A Decision Reversed

Poverty and disgrace are for the one who ignores instruction,
but one who heeds reproof is honored.
—Proverbs 13:18

There is that near you which will guide you.
O wait for it and be sure to keep to it.
—Isaac Penington, 1678

In my first year as executive director of a Quaker peace organization, I was enthusiastic about the Quaker practices for collectively discerning and following God's will. Many in the organization thought our focus was too scattered and unintentional. We felt the need to be more proactive. We reviewed the programmatic and financial condition of each program. I collected input about strengths, weaknesses, and dreams for the future. Then our board had a daylong planning retreat.

In the retreat, we felt strongly committed to the essence of our mission and ready to let everything else go. One of our programs was a summer family camp that had been meeting annually for thirty years. The camp evolved from its original mission of training peacemakers and activists to a focus on community building.

In the retreat we used the Quaker process of listening to each other in silence to discern the right path forward. Some felt a strong inner pull to let go of the summer camp and make room for other programs. We knew this decision would impact many families. Nevertheless our decision was to terminate the camp. To help with the transition, camp participants were allowed to run the camp on their own or take the program to another organization. As much as any other time in our board meetings, I felt that God was leading us in this decision.

Within a few days we received angry protests. Several emotionally charged meetings happened between campers and board members. A determined group of campers eventually managed to obtain a reversal from the board. The summer camp was allowed to continue under a new agreement, including increased volunteer leadership and a renewed focus on peacemaking and training for activism.

I felt confused and embarrassed. I thought God had led us in this decision. By backing down, were we now abandoning God's guidance? I was aware that the decision-making process and the following communication had been flawed. We had not followed the Quaker practice called "seasoning" (prayerfully sitting with a pending major decision for days or weeks before finalizing the decision), along with open communication and inclusiveness.

Now eleven years since that decision, the summer camp is still going strong under volunteer leadership. The board's decision empowered a group of program participants to become volunteer leaders. In retrospect we ask ourselves, "Would this revitalization have happened if the board had not decided to close the camp? Or was the board decision to close out of sync with God's will and plain wrongheaded?"

This experience suggests that following what we think to be God's guidance can be messy, but our attempts to be faithful can bear fruit, even if the results are quite different from what we imagined. I'm grateful for the ways that Christian community, and even conflict, can play essential roles in deepening our understandings of the right way forward.

Are we taking risks to be faithful in our decision making? Are we including all the people in the decision making who have a piece of the truth? Are we seasoning large decisions, to allow further light to be shed on them?

—Michael Bischoff of Minneapolis, Minnesota, is a lead consultant at Clarity Facilitation; he also facilitates discernment with a variety of religious and secular organizations.

You Didn't Listen to Me!

> Speaking the truth in love, we must grow up in every way
> into him who is the head, into Christ.
> —Paul, in Ephesians 4:15

It happens all the time. One leader accuses another of not listening. The defensive retort may be "I told them. . . . They looked right at me, but they didn't hear a word I said."

This scenario is frustrating. Sometimes different frames of reference make a meeting of meanings very hard to accomplish. Other times a misunderstanding results from personal perspectives about the meanings of words or the turning of a phrase that makes listening and understanding a real challenge.

The "not being listened to" accusation comes into play in other ways. In the process of working, learning, serving, and leading together, there are occasions when decisions are made. Because everyone does not think in the same way, or have the same preferences or strategies, or share the same vision for outcomes, collaborative decision making is often accompanied by creative tension. That makes listening critically difficult and important.

All of us want to get our way. When we don't get our way, we sometimes say that we were not listened to. Leaders can find ways to deal with such situations constructively.

First, the process should give everyone an opportunity to be heard. It is valuable to engage in active listening to insure clarity of the issue under consideration. A good technique is for chairs to repeat what the leader heard the speaker say, maybe concluding with "Have I heard you correctly?" It helps the speaker feel listened to. This procedure may prevent complaints and misunderstandings.

Second, when the "not listening" charge is made, the leadership may need to examine if ample opportunity was given to be heard. Perhaps the complaint is valid, and if so, as godly leaders we need to express regrets and apologize quickly, with sincerity and humility. On the other hand, if the complaint is unfounded, then the meeting should move ahead with the agenda.

In my experience, I have seen well-intended but overly dogmatic persons misuse the "not having been heard" plea. Yet at other times their complaints were valid. The process had not provided for enough examination by the members. An opposing view had not been respectfully heard.

As godly leaders we should make deep and respectful listening our goal, and then make appropriate amends when we fail. The Bible instructs us to speak the truth in love and also to listen respectfully to each other.

—Ed Boschman of Bakersfield, California, is national executive director of the U.S. Conference of Mennonite Brethren Churches.

God's Presence Through Music

> And whenever the evil spirit from God came upon Saul, David took the lyre and played it with his hand, and Saul would be relieved and feel better, and the evil spirit would depart from him.
>
> —1 Samuel 16:23

The air in the boardroom was tense and the trust level low. Those who ventured to speak chose their words carefully. It felt as though an evil spirit had invaded the boardroom and infested the minds and hearts of those seeking to discern and to do the will of God.

A fundamental policy issue was at stake, and the stakes were high. The positions seemed irreconcilable. The silence was nerve-wracking. Frustration, fear, and even anger were in the air. Unexpectedly somebody said, "Let's sing," and with a firm voice led out. The room slowly filled with the sounds and words of the powerful hymn they all knew by heart.

> Holy God, we praise your name; Lord of all, we bow before you.
> All on earth your scepter claim, all in heaven above adore you.
> Infinite your vast domain, everlasting is your reign.[2]

And then there was silence, but it was a different kind of silence. We felt less fear, less frustration, less tension. The atmosphere had changed as if a cleansing rain had descended upon us, as if God personally had come into our midst. Indeed, God had appeared in the form of music! The tone of the conversation changed. There was more listening, less harshness, and less judgment.

Boardroom veterans know that much more goes on in a meeting than is visible on the surface. Sometimes board meetings become perverted as if an evil spirit is at work. Sometimes something hurtful has been said. Sometimes it is an old grudge. Sometimes a difference of opinion becomes personal.

Words are not always enough to restore an open atmosphere. Words may actually make it worse!

Sometimes emotionally charged situations need an emotional response, like music. "Music," said Kahlil Gibran, "is the language of the spirit. It opens the secret of life, bringing peace and abolishing strife." This effect is also true in the boardroom. Music can calm behavior and heal the soul.

Perhaps the above illustration can inspire your board to look for new and unorthodox ways such as music to make God's presence felt in the many situations and moods that play out in the boardroom.

—Werner Franz serves as president and professor of practical theology at Centro Evangélico Mennonita de Teología Asunción (CEMTA) in San Lorenzo, a suburb of Asunción, Paraguay. He is a member of the Concordia Mennonite Church in Asunción.

Open Our Eyes, Open Our Ears

> When [Jesus] was at the table with them, he took bread,
> blessed and broke it, and gave it to them. Then their eyes
> were opened and they recognized him.
> —Luke 24:30-31

> Supposing him to be the gardener, she said to him, "Sir, if
> you have carried him away, tell me where you have laid him,
> and I will take him away." Jesus said, "Mary!" She turned
> and said to him in [Aramaic], "Rabbouni! [Teacher!]"
> —John 20:15-16

We thought we were on our way to a consensus when an opposing point of view was expressed. The boardroom atmosphere grew tense. "Why," we asked, "does someone always insist on bringing up alternate views? How can we be efficient and move ahead when there are so many opinions, or when several people insist on articulating the same position repeatedly. Why can't everyone just get on the same page?"

Our organization has a very diverse membership. We have made a deliberate effort to reflect that diversity in our selection of directors. Though we are committed to inclusion and diversity, there is no denying that a diverse membership makes arriving at a consensus more difficult. Sometimes these frustrations are so great that we ask whether it's all worth it.

Decision making in a heterogeneous environment takes more time. It requires vision, skill, patience, and an underlying commitment to strength in diversity. Taking the time to work through these differences can also enrich the end result and lead to deeper relationships.

Sometimes a short recess can relax the meeting's intensity. Informal corridor (or washroom) conversations can have an ameliorating effect. It can result in a deeper and a more objective understanding of differences. Yet a break can also have the opposite effect. It can result in increased polarization and entrenchment. Declaring a break is not a sure cure.

Compromise is a necessary part of corporate decision making. It is an indisputable fact of human nature that not everyone will arrive at the same conclusion. Call it give-and-take or organizational politics—some "negotiation" is necessary. It is not always bad. The challenge is to get beyond compromise, beyond being satisfied with the lowest common denominator, and arriving at a collaborative conclusion. That takes time and isn't always possible, but it remains an ideal.

We must also be aware that the Spirit may move through a minority voice. Sometimes an idea thought to be unworthy proves to be the discovery of the day. Not all minority opinions express the way to go, but each opinion is a piece of the whole and deserves to be processed thoughtfully.

We assume that a diverse body will have differences; yet to be viable, a body must have a common commitment that supersedes the differences. Directors must approach their board work with the belief that the whole body shapes conclusions, remembering that the board is the board together. At times compromise is not the way to go, but seeing and hearing a new way may actually come through a small voice. The board, in response to the Spirit, senses this and moves ahead courageously.

Arbitrating sincerely held differences taxes the spiritual resources of the group, especially the leaders. It calls for application of "the fruit of the Spirit"—"love, joy, peace, patience, kindness, generosity, faithfulness, gentleness, and self-control" (Gal 5:22-23)—as the guiding principle, being reminded that we are one in Christ.

The disciples' eyes were opened in the sharing of bread. Mary's ears were opened when approaching the one she thought had taken something from her. May we be open to each other in the sharing of bread and in listening to each other, especially those with whom we disagree, and in the process discover that God is creating "a new thing" in our midst (Isa 43:19).

—Ann Graber Hershberger of Linville, Virginia, teaches nursing at Eastern Mennonite University and leads cross-cultural semesters with her husband, Jim. She has served on various Mennonite Central Committee boards since 1996.

Round Pegs and Square Holes

Now there are varieties of gifts, but the same Spirit;
and there are varieties of services, but the same Lord.
—Paul, in 1 Corinthians 12:4-5

Let each of you look not to your own interests,
but to the interests of others.
—Paul, in Philippians 2:4

The report from our CEO did not come as a surprise. I had heard that not all was well with the performance of a senior employee. As in other situations I had experienced, it seemed that there was a poor fit between the person's skills, experience, or personality and the requirements of the position.

That fit should have been assessed at the time of appointment, but the selection process had been flawed. It now seemed clear that however fine the employee was as a person, we were confronted by a classic situation of a round peg trying to fit into a square hole. I could see the person being slowly diminished while at the same time the organization's ability to fulfill its mission was being compromised.

This kind of misfit may also arise when the leadership needs within the organization change or when an employee's personal circumstances, career goals, or family situation changes.

A round peg (the person) can be forced into a square hole (the position), but the optimal situation occurs for both the organization and the person when a good fit is achieved. A bad fit leaves the employee compromised and the organization unfulfilled, both less than they could be.

Yet our board was reluctant to make the hard decision to terminate. It could, members reminded themselves, result in conflict! The person might well be hurt; self-esteem would be lost! A wrongful dismissal suit might follow. A friendship might be at risk.

Boards want and need to be compassionate, but they are also required to provide effective executive leadership, and therein is the rub that calls for Spirit-led discernment. Termination can have negative or positive consequences. Both the organization and the person in question may be served better by a change, sensitively made.

Separation need not be seen as failure. There is nothing wrong with a round peg or a square hole. Both are of equal value, though of different shape and function. I have found, though not always immediately, that the person whose future was "freed by termination" has discovered a career shift that turned out well. The new fit was so much better. And in some cases I discovered their silent longing to be delivered from a poor fit.

So, when faced with what appears to be a poor fit, rally the courage to make a change and in the process free up both the person and the organization! And then determine that in the future there will be careful matching before a fit is attempted and sensitive monitoring of performance along the way. Ensure that if a misfit becomes evident, separation comes while both the board and the person are strong and able to find a better fit.

—Neil Janzen of Winnipeg, Manitoba, is chair of Mennonite Central Committee Canada. Earlier he was president and CEO of Mennonite Economic Development Association.

Mending Fences

> Be completely humble and gentle; be patient, bearing with
> one another in love.
> Make every effort to keep the unity of the Spirit through the
> bond of peace.
> —Paul, in Ephesians 4:2-3 NIV

Paul's words to the believers at Ephesus were intended to help a church that was experiencing conflict. He was pleading with them to reconcile with each other and make peace. The boards of Christian organizations sometimes face these same challenges. Paul's suggestions to the people in Ephesus can be useful for boards when conflict exists in their organization.

Pour yourselves out for each other in acts of love (cf. Phil 2:17). That's a difficult bit of advice for boards. Members come to meetings with thick dockets, full agendas, important business to conduct, and usually not enough time to finish their work. Performing acts of love are not on most written agendas. Paul nevertheless asks Christians to pour themselves out in acts of love for each other, especially during times of conflict.

As you start your next meeting, imagine what could happen if you welcomed God's outpouring of love on fellow board members, the staff, and the various stakeholders of the organization. That generous gift of love will reshape the agenda, inform decisions, and make peacemaking the business of the board. When the spirit of love permeates the entire culture, brokenness can be prevented, and for relationships already broken, reconciliation becomes possible.

Be alert to differences. Too often we'd rather not notice differences within the organizations that we govern. Differences tend to make us uncomfortable and can be hard to resolve. They can distract us from the agenda. They take up important board time.

Boards experience differences at any number of places. A misunderstanding may arise within the board itself, between the board and the administration, between the administration and staff, between staff members, and between the organization and its constituents. Paul implies that being alert to differences can prevent brokenness. If we ignore them, they can grow and become more difficult to resolve.

Be quick to mend fences. Sometimes tensions develop in organizations in spite of how alert and caring the board may be. Directors need to be committed to repairing what is broken, wherever that happens. Boards operate under time and financial constraints and on occasions make decisions that cause pain, such as a staff termination or increased fees. Because organizations are a complex blend of personalities and contrasting opinions, conflict is inevitable.

In a polarized world, boards nevertheless need to take the lead in peacemaking. They can set an example of transparency, explaining the reasons for their decisions, and asking for forgiveness when their actions have caused personal offense. On occasions it is necessary to invite an outside mediator to bring better closure to a conflict.

It is our God-given responsibility as board members to take the lead in creating communities of koinonia in the organizations we govern. We are its pastors, its caretakers, its governors, the ones who set the tone. As in Ephesus, we may not be able to eliminate all conflict or to develop a staff that is totally committed to the mission. But it is our responsibility to listen to the many voices that we serve and to create an environment of safety, respect, and agape love. Although our primary mission is centered on the people we serve outside of our doors, we need to be equally concerned with the internal mission: the well-being of the staff who are responsible to deliver the services of the organization.

—Gerald W. Kaufman of Akron, Pennsylvania, has been a clinical social worker and is author of *Freedom Fences*.

From Whence This Foul Odor?

> Why do you see the speck in your neighbor's eye, but do
> not notice the log in your own eye? Or how can you say
> to your neighbor, "Let me take the speck out of your eye,"
> while the log is in your own eye? You hypocrite, first take
> the log out of your own eye, and then you will see clearly
> to take the speck out of your neighbor's eye.
>
> —Jesus, in Matthew 7:3-5

After a long day at the office, I suddenly realized that it was time to pack my things and head for an evening dinner event, where I was to be the featured speaker. I looked forward to the presumed two-hour ride to unwind from the day and observe God's handiwork with the fall colors.

Suddenly I realized that I had miscalculated. Instead of a two-hour drive, it would take nearly three hours. Stepping on the gas pedal, I hoped to make up at least a bit of the time. I thought, "They can proceed with the meal, and I can speak when I arrive and eat later."

I arrived at the small town in central Pennsylvania. Seeing a church steeple, I quickly parked my car and ran up to the church entrance. It was locked. Seeing another church down the street, I ran there and yanked open the door. A men's prayer meeting was under way. Wrong again.

Panic-stricken, I looked around and was grateful to see someone: I asked for directions. My target, it turned out, was two blocks distant. I jogged to the destination, taking the shortest route possible, jumping over hedges and fences, all the while sweating profusely. Inwardly I was beating myself up for my poor planning that got me into this fix.

The host was relieved to see me and insisted that I have a quick meal while he made some final announcements. I was seated beside a gentleman when I became aware of the most awful foul smell surrounding him. I thought, "Doesn't he have the self-respect to shower before going into public?"

I finished my plate of food and took the podium, where the air was fresher. The rest of the evening went acceptably well. As I got back into the van for the return trip, I realized to my embarrassment that the foul smell had followed me. I looked down at my shoes, and behold, they were caked with dog droppings, presumably acquired while running through yards on my way to the church.

Misunderstandings and conflicts cannot always be avoided. But we can do some things to lower their frequency or to help manage them better. One is self-care. Leaders often act and work as if the world depends on them. To perform well each day, leaders need to take time for rest, inspiration, reflection, and physical exercise. I also set small goals for the day, asking for God's guidance. I think I know where I am going, yet my first need is the leading of God's Spirit.

When conflict arises, directors do well to examine their own heart first. In this case, they also need to examine their own shoes! That may be where the foul odor is coming from.

—Kevin King of Lititz, Pennsylvania, is executive director of Mennonite Disaster Service.

When Trust Is Lost

> God is our refuge and strength,
> an ever-present help in trouble.
>
> —Psalm 46:1 NIV

We had been so careful. We thought we had developed the team covenant so as to avoid the disappointment that hit us with all the force and unpredictability of an earthquake. Incredulously, the trust we thought we had built came crashing down around us with the painful betrayal of one of our number, wounding us all. Together we went through a cycle of confusion, anger, disappointment, shame, and a deep sadness as we realized what was happening.

Loss of trust is a serious blow to any organization. As people of faith, any major disappointment causes our reflection to return to something deeper than us and more unchanging than our fickle human nature. In times like these, we need something that is not shaken, not in the scandals of human drama.

And so, as people of faith have through the ages, we come to God in the midst of our disappointment, not to mask or hide our pain, but specifically because it is in communion with God that we gain perspective. We rediscover the One who is unchanging and unshaken even as we reflect upon our own shortcomings. The gift of such a season is that the turmoil draws us to the bedrock of our faith, even while we shed our own arrogant self-righteousness.

Specifically while the storms of organizational turmoil swirl around us, we not only find our refuge in God; we also find that God meets us right there at the point of our greatest fear and pain. And from that point of connection, God invites us to join the divine dance of God's purposes.

Because of this invitation, we are reoriented to look beyond the moment of discouragement and tap into a larger reality, to learn from our mistakes. This reorientation may call us to forgive others and ourselves for the shortcomings that caused the pain, and then chart a course to systematically rebuild the trust that was lost. Ultimately the goal is to find the path of reconciliation for all the relationships, for everyone's best interest. For such is the kingdom of God.

Especially amid such painful and discouraging situations, the invitation of God echoes through the ages, calling us to quiet reflection. In that holy space, God's voice comes through the noise of the urgent and the demands of the important, pointing us to where trust begins and hope resides.

In the midst of our deliberations as a board, may we find a posture in our spirit, and the collective positioning of our board, to hear the One who is whispering to us, "Be silent, and know that I am God! I will be honored by every nation. I will be honored throughout the world" (Ps 46:10 NLT).

—Terry Shue of Kidron, Ohio, is director of leadership development for Mennonite Church USA.

After a Long Struggle, the Gift of Peace

Let the peace of Christ rule in your hearts,
    to which indeed you were called in the one body.
And be thankful.
                                                —Paul, in Colossians 3:15

It was a precarious time. It was also a time of great possibility. The board representing the Mennonite Church and General Conference Mennonite Church was meeting in Nashville to decide the issue of merger, which had been under consideration for decades. The hour of decision had come. At this assembly, the church bodies would decide if this movement should result in the birth of a new entity.

Outside, it was hot and muggy. Inside, the comfort of the air-conditioned convention center belied an underlying uncertainty. "Are we ready? Will the hard work of creating a common vision and purpose in unifying two denominations come to fruition?"

As chair of the board, I was well aware of uncertainties looming in the minds of board members and delegates. Months of conversation across the church had contributed toward a growing sense of unity and of God's call to enter into a process of transformation. But some also had serious reservations.

There had been attempts to clarify some finer points of disagreement, including differing interpretations of the Mennonite Confession of Faith (1995). Some congregations were threatening to opt out if the merger went forward. An attempt to outline membership guidelines for the new denomination satisfied some; this effort raised fears in others, particularly those attuned to the differing cultural and historical practices that had shaped each denomination.

The biggest issue was homosexuality, about which there was a broad spectrum of positions in both denominations. Consideration of this question, a flashpoint for many, led to acknowledgment that the matter would require continued discernment and would not be finally settled at this convention.

As moderator of the assembly, I felt totally inadequate—perplexed in the first place about why I had been asked to serve in this capacity. Indelibly etched in my memory was the gathering a few months earlier, when the board met to make the final preparations for the summer assembly. The executive committee of the board met at an early hour to pray, to assess where we were—to prepare the board and ourselves for what lay ahead.

We felt the weight of what would be a momentous decision. The vote would be cast, yes or no. Do we unify, or do we go our separate ways? We came before God, realizing fully that the outcome was not in our hands. We had done our best. We had moved ahead in faith that God was doing a new thing. But we also were keenly aware that the delegates might reject the long-anticipated merger.

In quietness we embraced Paul's words to the Colossians, a Scripture from the theme text for the assembly: "Let the peace of Christ rule in your hearts, to which indeed you were called in the one body. And be thankful."

The Spirit's gift to us in that moment was the gift of peace. We experienced the indescribable sense that whatever happened, whichever way the delegates would decide, as a board we must now leave things up to God and the Holy Spirit.

Postscript—a confession: As a tangible reminder of this lesson in "letting go," I still carry in my Bible a slip confirming that the vote was "yes."

—Lee Snyder of Harrisonburg, Virginia, is president emeritus of Bluffton University and earlier served as vice president and academic dean of Eastern Mennonite University.

The Right Word at the Right Time

Let your speech always be gracious, seasoned with salt,
so that you may know how you ought to answer everyone.
—Paul, in Colossians 4:6

I was one of three speakers at a Conversations on Faith conference—in a series of meetings designed with the hope of resolving
some theological differences. Each speaker was assigned a topic with
a fifteen-minute limit. My assigned topic was biblical criticism. The
two speakers preceding me were quite forceful in rebuking biblical
criticism in the church. I knew that my presentation would reflect a
more moderate point of view. When I began to speak, I could feel my
knees shaking.

I was progressing through my prepared speech when I noticed
the timekeeper's red light. I finished my presentation even though
I was overtime. Then, to my surprise, the meeting broke out in
extended applause. It was a high moment for me. I was swept off
my feet, figuratively. I had not expected that kind of affirmation.
One person told me that it was my gentle, nonassuming manner
that brought the response. Another said that my message had reso-
nated with the group.

Paul's word to the Colossian church calls for a manner of speech
that is gracious. Gentle and loving words go far when there is conflict
and tension in the boardroom. Paul also says that our speech is to be
seasoned with salt. In the rabbinic writings, and in the writings of the
early church fathers, wisdom is associated with salt. Only after my
presentation did I realize that my words reflected the kind of speech
that the apostle Paul had in mind.

Boards must honestly face both the good and the difficult. They
cannot simply rubber-stamp the views of the CEO and management. When there is conflict within the board, it must be talked
about freely and openly. Too frequently we take the easy road of
withdrawal and talk to someone in the parking lot after the meeting. A healthier approach is to speak openly and honestly in the
meeting itself. Differences need not cut off communication.

The spirit and attitude with which we address one another
make a lot of difference. Gracious speech addresses the issue in a

manner that reflects honesty and kindness. Gracious speech is kind to persons, but clear and open on the issues. It does not circumvent the issue by confusing it with other issues. Speech that is seasoned with salt is perceptive. It is speech that arises from a reservoir of wisdom. When our words and meetings are seasoned with salt (Christian wisdom), we can work our way through differences.

Experienced board members can recall meetings seasoned with pepper (anger or pride) instead of salt! Instead of shedding light on the issue, harsh and accusing words resulted in dissension and hurt feelings. Sad to say, sometimes I have spoken with pepper. I can also recall board meetings where someone withheld insights for fear of offending others. The apostle Paul suggests that our speech should be gracious in manner and seasoned with wisdom (salt). It will enhance the board's conversation and help it work its way through the agenda.

—Paul M. Zehr of Lancaster, Pennsylvania, has served the Mennonite church as a bishop, teacher, and administrator.

Prayers

God, who created each of us with unique gifts and perspectives,
    who calls us to work together in harmony and peace,
    and who promises to heal and restore us when we fail,
we face the possibility of conflict today.

We confess that our motives may be mixed;
    sometimes we think our own way is better than another;
    and sometimes we honestly don't know.

At times we are threatened by the experience and wisdom of others.
When their viewpoints don't match ours,
    we judge them,
        suspecting that they may have their own interests at heart
        rather than the purposes we have been called to serve.

Forgive us when we mistrust and misunderstand each other.
Set us free to speak clearly, honestly, and lovingly.
Keep our hearts and minds fixed on the mission of our board.
Help us to honor each one's voice
    and to remember that you have called each board member
    to make a unique and important contribution.
Let our differing viewpoints be a catalyst to create a future
    that is stronger and more vibrant
        than any of us could imagine alone.

In the end, help us to speak with a single voice.
Unite us as members of one body
    so we may reflect the love of Christ
    and serve you with grace and peace in the world.

We pray in the name of Jesus, Prince of Peace. Amen.

—Marlene Kropf is associate professor of spiritual formation and worship, Associated Mennonite Biblical Seminary, and the former denominational minister of worship for Mennonite Church USA.

Let us pray. [*Silence.*]

We do not agree. Our stomachs are churning, our cheeks are warm, our hands are clammy. We are afraid of loud voices, of silent stares, of uncomfortable discussions.

All of these difficult moments we bring to you, God of creation and God of redemption.

We claim, however, that the Holy Spirit will abide in our noisy conversations and our silent moments. We plead for your Spirit of wisdom to reclaim our deeply held opinions and reshape them into genuine discernment. We accept our role as leaders to make difficult decisions, to speak the truth in love, and to lead [*name of the organization, church, nonprofit*] in a unified way. Help us to understand each other—our disagreements and our differences. Then, Holy Spirit, calm our anxious minds and bring us to a new place, where we honor each other and move forward together.

Amen.

—Dorothy Nickel Friesen has spent her professional career in the English classroom as teacher and the last twenty-eight years as a Mennonite pastor, seminary administrator, and conference minister.

Forgiving God, how many times we call upon you to help us, to guide us, even to heal us in our brokenness. We remember how Jesus Christ, in his own urgent prayer, asked for unity and oneness. That spirit often eludes us even as we yearn for it. From our separate thoughts and ideas, join us together in your Spirit. Amen.

—David Johnson Rowe is copastor of Greenfield Hill Congregational Church, Fairfield, Connecticut.

9

Meditations for Ordinary Times

What Is Vital? *R. Lee Delp*
Zero-Sum Versus Abundance, *Berry Friesen*
Keeping the Main Thing the Main Thing, *Beryl Jantzi*
Teamwork: A Fellowship of Endeavor, *Jonathan P. Larson*
Begin with the End in Mind, *Albert C. Lobe*
Words, Words, Words, *Lynette Meck*
God's Presence Permeates the Ordinary, *Willard Metzger*
Test the Spirits, *Cynthia Peacock*
Give Space for God—Everything Else Is Secondary, *Mary Raber*
Diversity Is Gift, *Carlos Romero*
Small Things Make a Big Difference, *Lee Snyder*
Faith, Hope, and Love, *Pat Swartzendruber*
Leadership for Generations, *Richard Thomas*
Jesus Invites Us to Rest in Him! *A. Richard Weaver*
Two Work Here, *Mel West*
Praise God for the Gift of an Ordinary Day, *David M. Wine*
Prayers

Introduction

Most boards yearn for the "ordinary" time. They see themselves as being constantly in the midst of white water and long for a quiet eddy away from internal and external pressures.

Neither organizations nor directors who lead them should be in a state of constant, unrelenting tension. There should be times when directors can back away from everyday pressures and focus on the future. Most boards don't take enough time to reflect. What

185

is going well? What can be learned about opportunities on the ever-changing landscape? What activities should be sustained? What should be concluded? What shows promise for future growth?

But ordinary time can also be dangerous. Instead of using their time to plan ahead, ordinary boards allow themselves to get drowsy, careless, or indifferent. Boards can become bored. They grow bored with the routine. In private moments they even find themselves wondering why there should be a board. Do they add any value? They lose their concentration, and worst of all, they begin to think of ordinary as their new normal. They may even resent it when presented with hard choices!

In ordinary times, directors may lose their concentration and fall behind the curve. While basking in a world of undeserved self-confidence, opportunity may be slipping through their fingers. Boards do well to be vigilant, being reminded that pride, inattention, and indifference go before the fall!

When asked, "What is a leader's first responsibility?" Max De Pree, author of numerous books on the topic, replied, "The interception of entropy."

For all their compassion, many nonprofit directors become passive: they are asleep at the wheel. They feel no sense of urgency. They fail to be sufficiently self-critical. They become risk-averse. In short, they surrender the very traits that have propelled them into greatness. Indeed, many directors see their role as being little more than serving as the CEO's cheerleader, instead of holding the staff accountable for outcomes.

In his little classic book *No Easy Victories*, John W. Gardner writes: "Organizations go to seed when people in them go to seed. And they awaken when the people in them awaken. The renewal of organizations and societies starts with people."[1]

The Scriptures, too, admonish us not to be slothful, as in Romans 12:11: "Do not lag in zeal, be ardent in spirit, serve the Lord."

Great organizations never rest on past laurels. They do not tolerate sloth or waste. They are continually reaching for a higher level of excellence.

Be happy, therefore, when times seem ordinary, but don't think of them as normal or even permanent. Do not allow sleep to overtake you, and do not allow yourself to become complacent and overconfident, feeling that you are exempt from trends and cycles. Do not be resentful or discouraged when your organization passes through choppy waters. Rather, use ordinary times to prepare for the challenges ahead.

Ordinary is the state an organization passes through between moments of glory and life-threatening uncertainty to do extraordinary things.

Select a meditation from this chapter that best speaks to the situation facing you. You may find it beneficial to page through other chapters, especially chapter 10, since themes in these chapters overlap. Feel free to inject your thoughts and adapt to your circumstances. Conclude with a prayer from the end of the chapter, again feeling free to adapt it. Some may want to repeat the Lord's Prayer in unison or sing a song together. Use silence and thoughtful pauses. Be relaxed and worshipful. Make it your goal to set a spiritual tone that will pervade the entire meeting.

What Is Vital?

> Now you are the body of Christ and individually members of it.
> —Paul, in 1 Corinthians 12:27

I stumbled upon a technique of summarizing and reviewing monthly business results in a short form that I called "Vital Signs." It gave me a quick summary of all the major business activities: cash flow, quality measures, operating ratios, bank covenant requirements, inventory levels, and receivables. For quick reference, it was all on one page.

An enterprise for which I was responsible had completed a record year. Sales, margins, inventory levels—everything appeared to be in good order, and all were happy! The human relations director suggested that we communicate our success with the employees so they could share the joy and feel thanked.

To our shock and disappointment, the opposite happened. Instead of joining in the celebration, employees told us that they felt overworked and underappreciated. One said he felt like an unimportant cog in a big wheel. We were taken aback. We had graded ourselves with an A, but the employees gave us an F. The vital signs had not given us the complete picture.

In its early days, the church understood itself to be the body of Christ. It consisted of many new converts in locations around the Mediterranean world. The apostles made the circuit to encourage and help develop these new believers. With Jesus no longer in their midst they understood that their work was done in the power of the Holy Spirit.

But as the years and now centuries have worn on, what called the body of Christ has changed. The church is now considered to be a building: "Look at our beautiful church." The church is regarded as an organization associated with a denomination, such as Episcopal, Presbyterian, Lutheran, Mennonite, or Baptist. Although our theology states that the church is the living body of Christ, our actions project a different definition.

I learned the hard way that an enterprise is more than the head office, the balance sheet, or a prestigious board of directors. An enterprise is its people working together to accomplish a mission.

Every enterprise is people. Yes, there are bylaws and buildings; there are goals and objectives and results to review. But people are collectively the essence of the enterprise and its mission.

How do you as a board view your organization? You undoubtedly talk about the results and plans and issues, but what about the people? How well do you know what they think, how they feel, what they are experiencing? Most important, how do they feel treated, and how do they treat each other?

Employee morale and commitment cannot be quantified or captured in the vital-signs summary, but they are an indispensable part of the picture and produce the results summarized in the vital-signs instrument.

In your next meeting, view your enterprise as a living organism, made up of people who are the everyday shoe leather that makes your mission and vision real. The way your volunteers and employees feel today shapes the way those whom you serve will feel tomorrow.

—R. Lee Delp of Lansdale, Pennsylvania, has served with many boards, both for profits and nonprofits.

Zero-Sum Versus Abundance

Give, and it will be given to you. A good measure, pressed
down, shaken together, running over, will be put into your lap;
for the measure you give will be the measure you get back.
—Jesus, in Luke 6:38

Life includes many lessons about scarcity. We learned some of
the first lessons around our family tables: there is only so much
ice cream in the bowl; the more you eat, the less there will be
for me. That lesson has been reinforced countless times over the
years. For some, it defines the essence of board leadership: allo-
cating scarce resources among competing needs.

Life also teaches us about abundance. This lesson points in
the opposite direction: the more you give, the more you get. Jesus
enacted the principle of abundance on the day he accepted the
loaves and fishes from the little boy, blessed them, and held them
up for the entire crowd to see. Miraculously, people who had been
hungry for fear of revealing their hidden caches of food made it
available for all to share. There was plenty, with extra left over.

Most of us have experienced this principle of abundance. Generosity by one prompts it in others. A humble confession by one
prompts confession in others. Love is like that too. As it is practiced, the supply increases!

This principle of abundance is not limited to intangibles. As
businesspersons know, some dollars spent are gone forever while
other investments return many times over. Even the economy is
not a zero-sum game!

In this passage, Jesus teaches that there are more resources
than we can imagine, and we can unlock that abundance when
we don't hoard what we have.

These principles of scarcity and abundance apply also to our
organization's approach to power. In a formal sense, power resides
with the board of directors and is delegated to the executive director. How should we think about that power? Is the principle of
scarcity or the principle of abundance more applicable? The answer
to that question will make a big impact on staff and on the experience of community members as they interact with staff.

If the principle of scarcity applies, the executive directors will make an effort to retain most of this limited commodity in their hands. As suggestions and proposals are debated within the organization and decisions are made, everyone will keep a close eye on who is gaining power and who is losing power.

But if the principle of abundance is applied, the executive director will assume that the supply of power will increase as staff members become more skilled, as the strategic plan is better aligned with the mission, and as creativity is unleashed. As suggestions and proposals are debated within the organization, the executive will seek to empower others and enable them to become stronger and influential contributors to the mission.

This surely is not a simple choice. Within the dynamics of organizational life, people sometimes hold to one principle and sometimes to the other, depending on what suits them. Recognizing these dynamics is part of the challenge of leadership, whether as a board director or as an executive director. It is decisive that we understand the principle of abundance and look for opportunities to apply it.

Jesus taught that life is not a zero-sum game. We can live and work in such a way that your gain does not come at my expense. May we live and work that way today.

—Berry Friesen of Lancaster, Pennsylvania, is an attorney who has served on several nonprofit boards and was executive director of the Pennsylvania Hunger Action Center, Harrisburg.

Keeping the Main Thing the Main Thing

> I have this against you, that you have abandoned the love
> you had at first. Remember then from what you have
> fallen; repent, and do the works you did at first.
> —The exalted Christ, in Revelation 2:4-5a

Stephen Covey, in *Seven Habits of Highly Effective People*, wrote, "Put first things first."[2] Later he restated it as "The main thing is to keep the main thing the main thing."[3] I like this quote. It is easy to remember, but it is not easy to accomplish. Becoming sidetracked and distracted in our personal goals and aspirations is all too familiar. This is true also in organizational life. We so easily forget the *main thing*.

In the Revelation to John, it was the church in Ephesus that was accused of falling prey to this lapse in focus. Individually, congregationally, and organizationally, we easily stray from our true calling unless we are committed to keeping our focus on the one thing that shines as a beacon and directs our decisions and actions.

A story is told of a seafaring village located at a point of land that jutted into the Atlantic Ocean. The seas were rough and the shoreline was rocky. Many ships and sailors were lost on the treacherous shore, unable to find safe harbor. So the community developed a team of expert seamen whose mission was to guide the ships.

They took things to the next level by building a lighthouse to warn ship captains of approaching danger. This had the effect of decreasing the number of rescue missions, causing the people of the village to become relaxed and distracted. They eventually became less concerned about their mission and calling to serve the seamen and their ships. They converted their boathouse into a social hall, to host parties and gatherings for the townsfolk.

One blustery night the town was celebrating at the social center, unaware that the lighthouse beacon had malfunctioned. Captains that had come to rely on the light to warn them of impending danger lost their bearings and ended up on the rocks. Scores of sailors died while the town reveled in the luxury of their social center. The next day the town awoke to the devastation of ruined ships and dead sailors on their shoreline.

Change is inevitable and can be good. But advancements in our environment and the routine of service can cause us to become less vigilant, even careless about our most basic mission. The lighthouse was a great advancement—as long as the light functioned as intended. Who is responsible for tending the "lighthouse" in your organization? I suggest that it is everyone's business. Our failure to maintain the most basic commitments, procedures, and safeguards can have tragic consequences.

As organizations grow and change everyone, both board and management need to be vigilant and focused on keeping the main thing as the *main thing*.

—Beryl Jantzi of Harrisonburg, Virginia, is a pastor and stewardship education director for Everence, a finance and mutual aid organization.

Teamwork: A Fellowship of Endeavor

> Do not think of yourself more highly than you ought, but
> rather, think of yourself with sober judgment, in accor-
> dance with the faith God has distributed to each of you.
> Just as each of us has one body with many members,
> and these members do not all have the same function,
> so in Christ we, though many, form one body, and each
> member belongs to all the others. We have different gifts,
> according to the grace given to each of us.
> —Paul, in Romans 12:3b-6a NIV

A dawning byword in the modern wisdom of organization—whether
corporate, community, or church—is the savvy strength of leadership
teams. Clustered skills of vision and logistics, varieties of tempera-
ments, and diverse styles of expression can make for bulwarked and
believable leadership. By contrast, leadership that teeters on only two
feet may provide short-term agility but will struggle for secure footing over the long haul.

A compelling image of this for me is set in northeast India,
where one of Asia's great rivers, the Brahmaputra, flows out of the
Tibetan highlands and swings down a valley of bamboo groves,
quiet villages, and rice paddies, on its way to the Bay of Bengal. As
a child growing up on a bluff overlooking the river, I would watch
the steamers and local vessels plying the currents and skirting its
sandbars. If my luck would hold on a sunny day, I could finagle my
way onto one of the dugouts or passing boats at the landing.

Navigating the river successfully called for three functions.
First was the person guiding the boat at the stern, the one of sharp
eye who would read the landmarks and the surface of the water
in choosing a route. At the prow stood another person, providing
motive power, driving the boat forward with a silvery bamboo pole.
Finally, there was a third person, whose task was to bail water, usually with a rusty can or, in dire straits, with cupped hands.

You can imagine the role that fell to me as a child. I didn't
know the vagaries of the river and how to read its many moods. I
did not have the physical frame and muscle required to lean into
the pole and make headway against heavy current. But I could

take the can or the shard of pottery lying in the ribs of the boat to lighten the craft and ultimately to prevent it from foundering.

This threesome working together could safely see a score of travelers to the far shore, or carry to market a load of dried fish or bags of rice. But if just one of these three failed at the assigned task, the entire operation would be in jeopardy. Taken together, the keen eye and experience of the one at the tiller and the brawn of the barebacked boatman who worked the pole would have no prospect of success if the child who was bailing allowed the boat to be overwhelmed by its leaks.

The effect of this awareness is that each respected and depended on the contribution of the others. It was a fellowship of endeavor that conferred dignity and significance to all who labored on the river. Together, they were a living unity. The rhythm of the bailing, the chanted song of the one leaning into the pole, and the darting eyes of the one who scanned the route and held the tiller—all these were a single, living whole.

Let each one, then, play their part with focused powers. Let each be honored for their life-giving contribution. And let the pulse of all our hearts be bound together, matching the rhythm of heaven's purpose here.

—Jonathan P. Larson of Atlanta, Georgia, is a pastor, writer, and storyteller.

Begin with the End in Mind

> For everything there is a season,
>> and a time for every matter under heaven.
>>> —The Teacher, in Ecclesiastes 3:1

> To retire [leave] when the task is accomplished
>> Is the way of heaven.
>>> —Lao Tsz

In June 1980, our family moved from India to Akron, Pennsylvania, where I served as the Asia Secretary for Mennonite Central Committee (MCC). By August, I was on the road for five weeks. Returning to the office tired, the executive secretary asked about the trip and my family. He clearly cared for us, and it helped. His final word was "Remember, begin this work with the end in mind." How I loved that job!

How does one know when it is time to leave the work to which one has felt called? A performance appraisal at the American International School in Hong Kong by parents, colleagues, board members, and students gave me a look at myself that was jolting. There was affirmation, and how I needed that!

But the suggestions for improvement left me shaken. It took a week for me to come to terms with what they identified as needing attention. On a long walk beside the ocean in Repulse Bay, I resolved to work at them. I served there for seven good years and left with good memories, feeling that I was valued.

I have spent twenty-one years as principal in different high schools, and twenty years with MCC and the global church. Never have I stayed longer than seven years, and here is why:

1. I know that my style and energy can grate. I work hard at seeing myself in the third person, looking in on my relationships and participation in meetings, watching for areas where I was not helpful.
2. Research suggests that it is advisable both for the welfare of the institution and the individual for a senior administrator to move on after seven to ten years, to allow for "new blood," new energy. I have found this to be true.

3. I fear developing a sense of entitlement. A university professor who threatened his board by reminding them "Consider all I have given" failed to acknowledge what had been given to him.

4. Having given a job everything I have, I want to leave on my terms, rather than being nudged out. Too many friends and colleagues have stayed too long and ended up bitter people.

5. Leaders are what they are. My style is assertive, to debate at the table, not after the meeting. This style has limitations. Folks in the institution deserve a new leader with another style.

6. It is lonely at the top. It takes courage, energy, humility, and generosity to listen and to hear; it takes even more wisdom to coach and confront.

How does one leave well? At the beginning of an assignment, I often find myself thinking that I will never want to give up this job.

In Wendell Berry's novel *A Place on Earth*, Mat and Margaret Feltner's only son, Virgil, was killed, and Mat found it hard to come to terms with his death. Margaret reminded Mat, "When we've lost it all, we've *had* what we've lost. . . . From the day [Virgil] was born, I knew he would die. . . . I'd brought him into the world that would give him things to love, and take them away. . . . When his death is subtracted from his life, what is left is his life."[4]

After seven years I take with me a host of good memories that sustain me and enable me to begin again "with the end in mind."

—Albert C. Lobe of Kitchener, Ontario, is a veteran worker with Mennonite Central Committee, North America; representative to Mennonite World Conference; and board chair of Conrad Grebel University College.

Words, Words, Words

> Be still, and know that I am God.
>
> —Psalm 46:10 NIV

I enjoy words. I like putting words together to express a thought, a feeling, a conviction. I like finding the right words to express humor or affection. I like reading other people's words. Board meetings rely heavily on words to communicate. We say them, we hear them, we read them, and we write them.

Words are good. Words enable us to hear and understand each other, to move projects and processes forward, to make decisions. But sometimes we tire of words. This was the sentiment expressed by a colleague: "I am so weary of words," she said, "weary of information. By the time I understand it, it is replaced by new information. Can't we just give words a rest? Just be quiet? Just listen to music? Or maybe just listen to the silence for a while?" There is value in silence, in times of few words or no words.

Well-known theologian and writer Frederick Buechner said, "If you have to choose between words that mean more than what you have experienced and words that mean less, choose the ones that mean less because that way you leave room for your hearers to move around in and for yourself to move around too."[5]

We live in a fast-paced and constantly changing world. Information abounds. We are told that more information has been produced in the last 30 years than during the previous 5,000.

In 2009, claims the Wireless Association, 1.5 trillion text messages were sent in the United States.[6] That's a lot of words!

Organizations are encouraged to fail fast, fix it, and move on. Donors and other constituents can be impatient. They may want to follow their money from point of receipt to point of distribution. If organizations are not quickly responsive, contributors' time and money will go elsewhere.

How do board members of charitable and religious organizations balance the reality of this fast pace of change with God's call to us: "Be still, and know that I am God"?

How do board members maintain the ability to move quickly in making changes and at the same time show care and compassion for those who are affected by their decisions, sometimes in life-changing ways, including job loss? How do board members respond when friends, relatives, pastors, church members, or other supporters critique the organization for making changes with which they do not agree?

"Be still," the Spirit calls. "Be still, and know that I am God." And from T. S. Eliot's poem "Ash-Wednesday" we hear:

> Where shall the word be found, where will the word
> Resound? Not here, there is not enough silence.[7]

Talking with and listening to each other is good. The Spirit of God comes to us as we talk respectfully and listen thoughtfully. But the Spirit also often comes in silence, at times when no words are spoken.

As boards of directors, we are often less adept at silence and more focused on words. Do we run our meetings as if everything depends on our words and activities, or do we also believe that God works in silence and stillness? What does it mean for a board of directors to "be still and know"?

—Lynette Meck of Akron, Pennsylvania, is associate executive director of Mennonite Central Committee.

God's Presence Permeates the Ordinary

> The kingdom of God is as if someone would scatter seed on
> the ground, and would sleep and rise night and day, and
> the seed would sprout and grow, he does not know how.
> —Jesus, in Mark 4:26-27

I have often failed to appreciate the presence and activity of God during board meetings. My inclination is to move quickly toward the business at hand. I feel an eagerness to get started. Productivity triumphs over spirituality. Efficiency requests swift focus.

When discerning the activity of God, I also tend to anticipate the spectacular. I look for God in the extraordinary. As a result I overlook the routine. I neglect the common. But the activity and presence of God is most often missed in ordinary times.

This was demonstrated for me during a routine, ordinary board meeting. There was nothing striking about the agenda. Many of the items were housekeeping in nature. The discussions seemed predictable. We all knew each other, so introductions were not necessary. But my desire to rush into the agenda was halted by a sense of responsibility: a need to value the people gathered for the meeting. I looked around the table and realized that we were not ready to rush into the agenda. So I requested that we go around the table and allow board members to welcome each other.

What followed was startling. People took turns sharing about significant changes that had occurred since our last meeting. Some told of significant family dynamics. Others commented on job changes. Some shared disappointments, and others expressed a sense of celebration.

Within five minutes a sense of community had developed. Vulnerability dismantled walls of defense. Openness produced an atmosphere of trust. Disclosure paved the way for open dialogue.

But perhaps more important, this experience reminded me of the breadth of God's activity. The routine overshadowed the spectacular. Everyone comes to the board table from a unique context, a unique experience, and a unique interaction with the presence of God.

Like the parable with which this meditation begins, God's presence permeates the ordinary. It supersedes the routine. While the farmer sleeps, the seed grows. An ordinary summer night becomes an environment for miraculous growth. In like manner, God is active in the ordinary of our lives. When we stop to recognize God's presence, we awaken to a new reality.

Ordinary times are filled with the activity of God. The routine is brimming with the presence of God.

As our board members shared their experiences, we became aware of the active presence of God in our midst. God does not require our cooperation to act. However, God desires to redefine our concept of the ordinary so that it includes routine divine activity.

We moved into our meeting agenda with a fresh realization that God was with us, and with it a new level of expectancy emerged.

—Willard Metzger of Drayton, Ontario, is general secretary of Mennonite Church Canada.

Test the Spirits

> For the Son of Man came to seek and to save the lost.
> —Jesus, in Luke 19:10 NIV

Violence and fighting are everywhere. Individuals fight and kill each other, and nations rage against nations. Human life seems to have little value, and we sometimes wonder about the meaning of our very existence.

I am from India; the words above are true for India, where for many years we have lived with the exploitation of the poor and weak. Our tribal people and others continue to flee cruel social systems and rural poverty, often winding up on the streets of Kolkata (Calcutta) or other big cities. We have become almost immune to their suffering.

Thirty-eight years of employment with Mennonite Central Committee India gave me many opportunities to become acquainted with people who were deeply committed to sharing the good news in word and deed. In their daily routines, and without fanfare, our staff quietly carried on God's work as Jesus had outlined it after his resurrection. These ordinary people inspired me again and again.

One such person was Dr. Suna, a tribal medical practitioner. (He was from what are known in India as "tribal" people, indigenous groups beyond the pale of even the Hindu caste system, often the most neglected by government officials and social organizations.) One day Dr. Suna invited me to visit his home village. The local god-man, surrounded by a large crowd, was telling his listeners that he could cure any illness because he was blessed with magical powers. He told the crowd that if they refused to give Dr. Suna what he asked for his services, a curse would come upon them.

Illiterate and superstitious, his tribal listeners were easily exploited by this con artist. Whenever they went to the god-man for a medical cure, they gave him what they could, a chicken or a few grains of rice, which they desperately needed themselves. They were so immune to this kind of exploitation that it never occurred to them that they were gaining no medical benefits in exchange for the precious food items that they had foolishly given to the god-man.

Suddenly the god-man noticed Dr. Suna at the edge of the crowd, engaged in conversation with a few people. Afraid that his profession and income might be in jeopardy, the god-man energetically began telling the people to beware of Dr. Suna because he would ask them to take medicines that would force them to change their religion! Hearing that, we soon left the crowd, not wanting to stir things up.

Later that week the god-man sent for Dr. Suna, explaining that his wife was seriously ill and his own magical powers were not working. Dr. Suna willingly served the impostor and helped her to be admitted into a hospital. Three weeks later she had fully recovered.

The god-man gave up his profession and became Dr. Suna's assistant. Together they introduced a mobile health unit that offered additional medical services to the community. The entire village benefited from Dr. Suna's generosity. Children started attending the public school that Dr. Suna had nudged the government to open. The infant mortality rate dropped, and mothers began giving their children nutritious food. The good news for the tribal villagers came in another form. They were no longer victimized by a con man.

As stated in 1 John 4:1, boards and managers of faith-based organizations need to "test the spirits to see whether they are from God." Many false prophets offer their alternatives, and leaders are wise to heed the warning that Jesus gave his disciples: "Be wise as serpents and harmless as doves" (Matt 10:16).

—Cynthia Peacock of Kolkata (formerly Calcutta), West Bengal India, is director of Mennonite Central Committee India and chairs the Mennonite World Conference Deacons Commission.

Give Space for God—Everything Else Is Secondary

> Let no one despise your youth.
>
> —Paul, in 1 Timothy 4:12a

Do you ever wonder, "How on earth did I get picked for this job?" Apparently Paul's youthful colleague Timothy did. It's easy to imagine him protesting, "But I'm only a kid!" as he faced the problems of guiding the church at Ephesus.

Ephesus was a tough post. Its economic life was tied up with worship at the great temple of the goddess Artemis, and the city was known for its religious prostitution and occult practices (see Acts 19). A Christian leader there would have to deal with a worldly international community, and sometimes Timothy just didn't feel up to it. The sophisticated Ephesians intimidated him. Maybe his voice cracked when he tried to sound authoritative. Maybe they questioned the decisions he made. He probably felt very lonely. Couldn't Paul find somebody else for the job and let him back out?

I can sympathize with Timothy, not because of my youth, but because I'm the only foreigner on the board of a Ukrainian theological school, and until recently I was also the only woman. Fortunately my colleagues don't look down on me as the Ephesians likely did with Timothy. They're good men and treat me with courtesy. Nevertheless, I sense barriers between us that make us feel awkward and annoyed with one another.

For example, they sometimes come across to me as typical "Soviet types"—opaque, authoritarian, and completely clueless. On the other hand, I know I often blurt out my opinions in a way their wives would never do. From there it's a short step to "despising"— judging and rejecting one another for qualities we can't do anything about, such as age, gender, cultural background, or national origin.

Worse yet, we can end up despising ourselves and assuming that we have nothing to contribute simply because we are who we are. Even though I was invited to my present position, I sometimes doubt that I belong there, simply because I am a foreign woman. Shouldn't they look for someone with whom they have more in common, who could communicate more easily?

Surely it's wise to consider humbly whether we're qualified for a particular job. Sometimes, however, it's all too easy to disqualify ourselves for the wrong reasons. Apparently some of the Ephesians thought Timothy was too young to deserve their respect, and he was on the point of agreeing with them. But youth is not the point. Timothy and the Ephesians forgot that our sovereign God puts us where we are for a purpose, no matter what our age or station in life!

Therefore Paul's solution is first of all to give space for God to work. Even in sophisticated Ephesus, his advice to Timothy is the basic stuff of Christianity: Don't worry about what other people think of you. Concentrate on your walk with Christ. Speak and act like a servant of God. Work on becoming an example of love, faith, and purity (1 Tim 4:12). Study Scripture together (v. 13). Faithfully practice your spiritual gift because God gave it to you and expects you to use it (vv. 14-15). Make sure that what you teach is reflected by the way you live so that you and others will be blessed thereby (v. 16)!

Like Timothy, our board work has its challenges. In low moments we ask ourselves, "Are we up to it?" We may be tempted to disqualify ourselves because we're young or old, male or female, Ukrainian or American. But Paul says those things aren't the real point. He tells us, "Resist despising yourself and others! Instead, practice being the servant that God created you to be, and trust God to take care of the results."

—Mary Raber of St. Louis, Missouri, teaches church history and subjects in theological schools in Ukraine and Russia through Mennonite Mission Network. She is a member of St. Louis (Missouri) Mennonite Fellowship.

Diversity Is Gift

> There are different kinds of gifts, but the same Spirit dis-
> tributes them. There are different kinds of service, but the
> same Lord. There are different kinds of working, but in all
> of them and in everyone it is the same God at work.
> —Paul, in 1 Corinthians 12:4-6 NIV

"Diversity is a gift, not a problem," a friend of mine used to say. But the reality is that we live in a culture where differences are emphasized more than common core beliefs. Culture influences our institutions and the way we do our work.

In the Corinthian passage quoted above, the apostle Paul calls for unity in the midst of diversity and for the community to understand itself as one body. He begins by reminding us that although we have a diversity of gifts and ministries, there is only one Spirit and one Lord. I wonder how the diversity of gifts and unity of spirit are reflected in our work? As a board, do we intentionally take time to look at the various gifts and experiences that members bring and how they interact with each other? How does that diversity strengthen the work of the board?

Understanding diversity as a gift also compels us to ensure that each person contributes. How are the contributions of board members valued and recognized? Has the board developed a culture where all opinions are actively sought? As you reflect about your meetings, are there members who never speak a word?

Paul's message to the Corinthian church is as real today as it was then. Aware of divisions and problems among them, he offered counsel on how they could work together. In these verses, Paul outlines a number of principles to use in team building.

- Acknowledge the diversity of gifts.
- Everyone has something to contribute: find out what that is.
- Since God has provided us with individual gifts, the use of our gifts should ultimately help build God's kingdom.
- In a team, every person is important, and no one should feel or act as if they are better or more indispensable than others.

- Invite contributions from persons from whom you least expect to hear. Make sure that the input of everyone is solicited and welcomed.
- Team members need to care and respect each other. There will be diversity of opinions, but respect must always be the norm.
- Empathize with others; board members need to know how to cry together and how to laugh together.
- Remember that the diversity of gifts is intentional. God made and created each one of us as unique.

Former football coach Lou Holtz said that the answer we give to three questions will determine our success or failure:

1. Can people trust me to do my best?
2. Am I committed to the task in hand?
3. Do I care about other people and show it?

If we can answer all three questions with yes, we will not fail.

God has given us diversity of gifts, has called us to work as one, and has blessed us by providing us with the opportunities to be involved in God's mission. How strong a team is your board?

—Carlos Romero of Goshen, Indiana, is executive director of Mennonite Education Agency.

Small Things Make a Big Difference

> Humility is sometimes merely the knowledge that something
> is going on that you are too spiritually opaque to get.
> —Mary Rose O'Reilley, *Barn at the End of the World*

I have been associated with church organizations most of my life, both as a board member and as an administrator. I am convinced that God calls us as individuals to a work larger than ourselves. At times the sheer daily-ness of the work seems to get in the way: the deadline for a federal report, a financial crisis, an unexpected resignation, a disgruntled constituent, a donor who threatens to withhold contributions because he disagrees with an administrative or board decision.

Most of the time these examples belong in the category of the mundane. This is the stuff of our lives. Being called of God does not mean living on some lofty plane. Our calling, as Kathleen Norris reminds us, "does not grant access to all the answers but means contending with hard questions, thankless tasks."[8]

Sometimes, though—bursting through the tasks that prescribe our every day—we catch a glimpse of the mysterious. There are those times of unexpected insight, a transcendent moment in which the ordinary is transformed into the extraordinary. This happened one day when a young woman introduced herself to me at a national church convention. I recognized her name and was pleased to meet Brenda in person, since I had become aware of her in my role as academic dean at Eastern Mennonite University.

Several years earlier, I had telephoned Brenda to explore future interests in a university appointment. For me, it was all part of the job—the recruitment and encouragement of qualified Christian faculty. Later she told me her story. The day I had called was just when she and her copastor husband were beginning to ask out loud, "What next?" That morning at breakfast, Brenda told me, they had just "named to each other" that it was time to begin asking God how long they should stay in their current ministry. "So we prayed that prayer that morning," Brenda recalled. "On that very day, your call came," seemingly out of the blue. "I was blown away. The timing of your call just seemed to be no coincidence."

There in the convention hallway between sessions, meeting and greeting old friends, I was taken aback by Brenda's account. I had long forgotten my call to her. I was humbled again by the evidence that small things make a difference, that the Holy Spirit's work is often inscrutable and behind the scenes.

Just picking up the phone that particular day, attending to yet one more task, proved to be an act of obedience to some inner prompting about which I had no clue. It makes me laugh, this confirmation that something is going on beyond what we can fathom. I was reminded that even the most mundane efforts can have startling consequences.

"Pay attention to the nudges," I often tell myself. To board members, leaders of the church, and those serving the mission and vision of their organizations: Do not underestimate the power of the Spirit in the seemingly insignificant. In the daily routine, in the midst of imposing or trivial tasks, step back. Know that you are participants in a holy calling, a part of something at times too large for us to see.

—Lee Snyder of Harrisonburg, Virginia, is president emeritus of Bluffton University and served as moderator for the Mennonite Church USA in 1999–2001.

Faith, Hope, and Love

> If I speak in the tongues of men or of angels, but do not have
> love, I am only a resounding gong or a clanging cymbal. If I
> have the gift of prophecy and can fathom all mysteries and
> all knowledge, and if I have a faith that can move mountains,
> but do not have love, I am nothing. If I give all I possess to
> the poor and give over my body to hardship that I may boast,
> but do not have love, I gain nothing.
>
> —Paul, in 1 Corinthians 13:1-3 NIV

On a visit to Washington, D.C., I heard Nancy Pelosi address an audience and use the familiar passage from 1 Corinthians 13 as her text. "And where," she asked, "is hope found? It is located between faith and love." I was inspired by her hope-filled spirit as she—a devout Catholic, the daughter of a former Baltimore city mayor, and then U.S. Speaker of the House of Representatives—legislates health, dignity, and respect for all.

I reflected further on the Corinthian passage: "And now these three remain: faith, hope and love. But the greatest of these is love" (1 Cor 13:13 NIV). What is the role of faith, hope, and love in my service as a board member?

Faith is a quality that emerges as we live within structures and relationships. From simplistic to highly complex, we rely on tools like form and structure for a multitude of human endeavors. I feel blessed to live in a country where religious, social, and business entrepreneurship is encouraged to flourish and grow. We are free to create new forms and structures as they are needed.

In many countries, the faith-based nonprofit sector does not exist. I have spoken with leaders who are struggling to create these institutions for the benefit of their people. When given the opportunity, people will create forms and structures to benefit others.

I have faith in institutions and structures as vital vehicles for accomplishing much for many. I have faith in the goodwill of people, created in the image of God, with capacity to love their neighbor and care for the earth.

Hope, sandwiched between faith and love, is an essential quality when a flourishing mission and purpose is not yet in sight. Hope is essential when an organization is about to be formed and has not yet attained stability or full support.

Hope keeps me engaged and motivated when obstacles impede overarching aims of our organization or when conflicts obstruct a way forward. My hope is renewed as I remember leaders who had faith to develop and risk innovation. My hope is renewed as I reflect on how others will benefit from what we are creating.

My personal hope reservoirs are filled as I mediate and read Scripture daily, through regular participation in circles of listening and speaking, and in the humor and fun of relationships. These experiences stimulate and make my board work more productive and enjoyable.

Love is the quality that allows me to respect myself in ways that permit me to celebrate and engage in the goodness around me. In his book *Made for Goodness and Why This Makes All the Difference*, Archbishop Desmond Tutu writes: "The impulse to care, the instinct for goodness, is a shining thread woven into the fabric of our being. . . . We cannot alter our essence. We are made by God, who is goodness itself. We are made like God. We are made for goodness."[9]

As a board member, I experience deep love for those who are serving and receiving benefit from the mission of the organization. God's love, the richest example of true love, creates, sustains, and unconditionally remains.

My love, while never perfect, results in great joy as I watch others improve their quality of life and reach incremental goals. Love is the basis of my service. Our work as board members—when well grounded in faith, hope, and love—will flourish and remain.

—Pat Swartzendruber of Harrisonburg, Virginia, volunteers at Eastern Mennonite University and serves on the board of Everence, a financial and mutual aid organization.

Leadership for Generations

> Lord, you have been our dwelling place in all generations.
> Before the mountains were brought forth,
> > or ever you had formed the earth and the world,
> > from everlasting to everlasting you are God.
> > > —Moses, the man of God, in Psalm 90:1-2

> He established a decree in Jacob, and appointed a law in Israel,
> which he commanded our ancestors to teach to their children;
> that the next generation might know them, the children
> > yet unborn,
> and rise up and tell them to their children.
> > > —Psalm 78:5-6

The theme "generation to generation" is prominent in the Scriptures. God assures us of God's leading in generations past and also describes a more-recent presence and leading to the future. We are reminded that future generations will look to us as the ones who went before them and on whose legacy they will build. That makes our meeting important, knowing that our decisions impact not only us, but also generations yet unborn.

The apostle Paul reminds Timothy to follow the example of his grandmother and mother. Scriptures teach us to learn from the mistakes of Israel so they are not repeated. We desire to make wise choices that build positive bridges to the future. Kingdom building is not by our own might but by the power of God. So in this meeting, we open ourselves to God's wisdom and leading.

To discern and follow God's leading, we need to view the board's governance work as spiritual leadership. "Worshipful work" focuses on the big questions. It is clear about its vision and the establishment of a strategic direction that advances the mission to which we are called.

As a governance board, we resolve to keep what some call the "fifty-year vision" in front of us, to help us make decisions today that provide options for future boards and administrators. In so doing, we will discern the way of God and leave a good legacy, keeping both today and future generations in our common vision.

Philosopher Edmund Burke saw civilization as a partnership of generations "between those who are living, those who have died, and those yet unborn." Burke and the Bible agree that we have entered this world in debt to our ancestors. Each board meeting is, therefore, more than receiving reports and monitoring performance. The choices that boards make should build on the founders' vision, the history of the institution, and include spiritual discernment of a desired future. Out of our past, we can discern a useable future, as described in Isaiah 51:1: "Listen to me, you who pursue righteousness and who seek the LORD: Look to the rock from which you were cut and to the quarry from which you were hewn."

The founders of the school where I am superintendent had to choose between buying a full tract of land or purchasing only half the property. They wisely decided to buy more than was presently needed and by so doing made opportunities available for future students that otherwise would not have been possible.

Retelling this story has empowered our board to be futuristic in its decision making. The 1955 LMS class motto "Forward in Faith" encourages us to build bridges from the past to the present, always with a vision for our future.

The open, discerning leadership of the governing board sets an example for staff members as they implement the vision and mission. Staff is empowered by the leadership of the governance board. The board's leadership is the single most important factor in an organization. Its leadership reflects careful spiritual discernment at all levels, starting with leadership as modeled by the governing board.

May it be said of us, as of King David, that we served the purposes of our generation well, knowing that in so doing we leave a positive legacy for generations who follow. To God be all glory!

—Richard Thomas of Lancaster, Pennsylvania, is superintendent of Lancaster Mennonite Schools and moderator-elect of Mennonite Church USA.

Jesus Invites Us to Rest in Him!

Come unto me, all you that are weary, . . . and I will give you rest. Take my yoke upon you, and learn from me; for I am gentle and humble in heart, and you will find rest for your souls.
—Jesus, in Matthew 11:28-29

While serving with medical missions in East Africa in the 1960s and '70s, I soon learned that I was considered *Mzungu*, which in Swahili means "dizzy"! Tanzanians saw us Europeans and Americans as running around dizzy, nearly out of our minds. We were always in a hurry, often destroying relationships as we went about our daily work like fixing generators, water pumps, and leaky plumbing and treating patients in the hospital. We were not seen as contemplative people, who would take time to reflect on the gifts of the day, relationships, or creation and God.

In the Scripture verse quoted above, Jesus invites all to experience wholeness by resting in him. Implied in this invitation is the call to relax and still our frenzied spirits and find rest for our soul.

In the old main entrance to Johns Hopkins Hospital in Baltimore is a fourteen-foot-tall solid white marble statue of Jesus, standing with open arms to welcome all. Thousands have passed by this statute, given by people from Denmark in the late 1800s. As I watched people pass that lovely sculpture, I noticed that some touched the feet or toes of Jesus, and others made the sign of the cross as they passed. Some even kissed the feet of Jesus. It is easy to see the statue and miss hearing the words of Jesus, "Come to me . . ." What a difference this invitation can make in the lives of the people who touch and kiss those feet.

In an article in *Spiritual Life*, Janet Ruffing writes about resisting the demon of busyness, which interferes with our relationships with people and with God. She calls busyness an addiction. We feel good being busy. The temptation is to become intensely anxious and restless if we have nothing to do. Ruffing adds: "This busyness in our Western culture supports the ever-escalating levels of violence. When we are too busy, we become not only uncaring but [also] volatile and violent. When anyone or any circumstance interferes with our self-importance or level of productivity, the urge is to erupt in some form of aggression. Emotionally, we become irritable and angry."[10]

As one of the *Wazungu* (dizzy, aimless wanderers), I noticed that, in the minds of Africans, we could soon erase all the good we had done by one angry, impatient outburst, even if it was for saving someone's life.

Jesus invites us to rest in him! How do busy directors do that? How do they bring this new spirit with them into the boardroom? Here are two simple suggestions:

1. *Be present to the moment.* This is probably the best definition of being contemplative. Most spiritual masters and teachers tell us that if we pay full attention to the thing at hand, we experience a sense of delight and serenity. We achieve this by a life lived in relation to the One we serve.

2. *Retreat from our daily routine.* When we retreat to quiet places, our sense of priorities begins to align itself with God's desires for us. Turning off the telephone, cell phones, and computers can help us to be in touch with our real value to God. This choice reduces the ego stroking that comes from being always available, always busy, and always dizzy!

—A. Richard Weaver of Lititz, Pennsylvania, is a retired missionary physician who serves as a spiritual director and retreat leader with Kairos School of Spiritual Formation.

Two Work Here

> For where two or three gather in my name, there am I
> with them.
>
> —Jesus, in Matthew 18:20 NIV

I was in Costa Rica to learn Spanish. Each afternoon I went for a walk in the beautiful countryside. The dark green and waxy leaves of the coffee plants sparkled in the tropical sun. I do not care for coffee as a drink, but I love the people who raise and pick the coffee. A valley whose hillsides are filled with contour-planted coffee is as lovely as a garden landscaped by professionals.

Water gurgled through the irrigation pipes that skirted the road. A flock of bright-green tropical birds took noisy flight from a flame tree as I passed by, scolding me for having disturbed them. Two bright-eyed children playing in their front yards giggled at my effort to speak to them in Spanish, then fled into the security of their little house. Their mother ceased her mopping to glance out at the stranger among them. A half-grown pup stood guard by a banana tree to make certain that I did not leave the road.

Then my eye was drawn to a lean-to shop at the side of the path. It was perhaps ten feet by forty feet, made of crude lumber and tin. The front had no wall, and as I came closer, I saw wooden bedsteads for sale. They were hand carved and a bit crude, but sturdy and with a unique air of elegance.

The carpenter came to the front, and I explained to him that I was not there to buy, but interested in him and what he did. This comment brought a tour of the shop. He used rough timbers with the bark still on two sides. His tools were simple, and the work was very labor intensive. With great pride he showed me a corner shelf he was making for his wife.

I asked him how many worked in the shop. He replied, "Dos." Two worked in the shop. I looked around for the other person. Smiling, he pointed to himself and said, "Uno [one]." Then he pointed upward toward the heavens and said, "Y Dios [and God]." He and God worked in the shop. Reaching for a piece of rough lumber, he said, "Dios." God provides the materials. Pointing to a finished bed, he said, "Yo y Dios [I and God]." God made the wood. The carpenter made the beds. Two worked in that shop.

His theology was simple and yet profound. Pondering it as I left, I thought of the Old Testament and how our spiritual forebears saw the hand of God at work in all that happened. Sophistication and "progress" tend to take us away from this feeling of relationship with the Eternal. I have visited many production plants that hired thousands of people, but never has the participation of the Almighty been so acknowledged.

How do we as trustees of a faith-based organization bring our own spiritual values into the boardroom and its discussions and decisions? How do we translate the values that we hold dear in our private and spiritual lives into policies that are best for the organization and for the people they are meant to serve?

How many serve on our board?

—Mel West of Columbia, Missouri, is a retired United Methodist pastor and board service veteran for nonprofits such as Heifer International and Habitat for Humanity International. He is founder of PET (Personal Energy Transportation) Project, providing hand-cranked wheelchairs to leg-handicapped persons worldwide.

Praise God for the Gift of an Ordinary Day

I've seen and met angels wearing the disguise of ordinary
people living ordinary lives.

—Tracy Chapman

I am fond of saying, "Praise God for the gift of an ordinary day!"
Isn't just an ordinary day about perfect? If it is ordinary, there are
no deadlines, no huge stress points, no ill health, no major decisions, nothing requiring change; nothing demanding us to be anything other than who we are! And isn't that just about the best gift
any of us can have?

Upon deeper reflection, we certainly realize that an ordinary
day does not exist. Every day comes with its challenges and miracles if we just look and pay attention.

Yet we often misplay this wonderful gift of the "ordinary." We
plod through our days hardly looking, hardly feeling, and anxious
when our ordinariness might change. Or we look backward with
regrets, disappointment, and reliving our past. So we miss the miracle of just an ordinary time in our lives when we can rejuvenate,
relax, pay attention to what is happening now, and simply enjoy.

Organizations are like us! We have times as boards and managers that demand our fullest attention—crisis moments of great consequence, paradigm-changing events, or financial results that create
a sense of urgency. Often, however, we are in a level period, a period
that feels ordinary, and our organizations and boards become predictable and perfunctory. The agenda seems light, and some might
even say it is boring. In those times, let's remember to do two things.

First, let's be thankful! What a wonderful gift to be in a leveling
period organizationally, when the pressures are reduced for awhile
and all seems to be humming along! We need these times. The resting points in our lives—both as individuals and organizations—create necessary space for us to rejuvenate and ready ourselves for the
next challenges we know we will face. No person or organization
can run indefinitely at fever pitch. Let's welcome these opportunities to live fully in this moment.

Second, let's remind ourselves that no ordinary time really exists.
Even though times may feel "relaxed," we know that every deci-

sion we make and action we take is building toward a future and is beset by uncertainties. Yes, there are times of lessened pressures, changes, or challenges. In terms of faithful living to God's call, however, ordinary is an oxymoron. Every decision made or not made is building our future. Every action taken or not taken is doing the same. The routine, usual, and customary events are opportunities to set even more time aside to discern the future together, to set forth an appropriate vision and mission for our organizations, to clarify our direction and intent. We dare not miss these rare times when our organizations are ordinary: they afford us the best possibilities to create a Spirit-led future. What a wonderful gift!

Let's use these so-called ordinary times to create even more time on our agendas for discernment, to be led by God's Spirit. It is these opportunities that can best shape our future into more perfect alignment with God's direction and call for faithfulness. Let's not wait until a crisis to discern and act. Blaise Pascal wrote: "Small minds are concerned with the extraordinary, great minds with the ordinary."

—David M. Wine of Overland Park, Kansas, is president and CEO of MAX, a faith-based insurance company, and served as moderator of the Church of the Brethren in 1996–97.

Prayers

God who showers new mercies upon us each morning,
    whose faithfulness extends to every day and night,
    and to every time and place,
we give thanks for your sustaining presence
    in each moment of our lives.

When nothing extraordinary is happening
    and we are simply showing up,
    being responsible,
    fulfilling our obligations,
    caring for each other and our world,
we are grateful for the strength that keeps us on course
    and for the opportunity to be about your work in the world.

Help us to see the beauty of the ordinary:
    to recognize that small daily acts of love make a difference,
    that doing good work honors you,
    and that conscientious care in humble duties is a witness to
    a watching world.

Keep us alert to surprises in ordinary times,
    to the new ways you may want to lead us
    and to the fresh guidance of your Spirit.
Do not let us become complacent,
    but keep us awake, always listening and watching for your call.

We pray in the name of Jesus of Nazareth,
    the One who walked humbly among us
    and who showed us day by day how to serve and love you
    with our whole heart, soul, and mind. Amen.

—Marlene Kropf is associate professor of spiritual formation and worship, Associated Mennonite Biblical Seminary, and the former denominational minister of worship for Mennonite Church USA.

Spectacular, creating, wondrous God, we pray this simple prayer of thanksgiving in this ordinary time for our board. We are not in crisis—hallelujah! We are not in the middle of a CEO search—great! It is, quite simply, a time of harvest—of gathering and savoring the fruits of our labor.

Our prayer is that we will not fall asleep, get lulled into routine, or smugly rest on our laurels. Keep us in your Spirit so that we use this ordinary time, this normal and usual time, as preparation and openness to new things.

Ever awake God, we embrace this ordinary time as a gift from you, and we treasure it like a priceless gem.

Amen.

—Dorothy Nickel Friesen has spent her professional career in the English classroom as teacher and the last twenty-eight years as a Mennonite pastor, seminary administrator, and conference minister.

∽

Extraordinary God, be with us in our ordinariness. You challenge us to be perfect, but most days are unexceptional. Keep us from apathy, smugness, or self-satisfaction. Help us to see each day as worthy of our best. We may not always dwell at the mountaintop, but even in our valleys may we rejoice in the privilege of life and service. Amen.

—David Johnson Rowe is copastor of Greenfield Hill Congregational Church, Fairfield, Connecticut.

10

Meditations to Seek Wisdom and a Deeper Spirituality

Introduction

In a fascinating book *If Aristotle Ran General Motors*, Tom Morris suggests that effective corporations have cultures that are characterized by deep wisdom and courage. Deep wisdom, according to Morris, is the sense of the right strategic and ethical thing to do. Courage, he mused, is the will to do it! But how does a board cultivate wisdom?

Directors are busy people. Most do their work over and above their "day job." They burn the candle at several ends, neglecting themselves and matters of the Spirit. The danger in this type of living, in the poignant words of songwriter Philip Brooks, "is that someday we may wake up and find we have been busy with the husks and trappings of life—and have missed life itself."

Governing boards can spend significant time in rearranging their agendas, discovering best practices, and improving their board competence and governance technique. Although these are important, the message of this book is that boards deepen the quality of their work and add value as they also make room for the spirit that undergirds meetings and the work that flows from them.

Much of what goes wrong in the boardroom, certainly much that distracts from wholesome relationships and meaningful exchange, can be traced to a lack of spirituality. A healthy spirituality can compensate for bad technique, but nothing, not even the best technique, can compensate for an unhealthy spirit.

This final chapter offers practical suggestions for how a board can bring spiritual resources to bear on their deliberation.

When boards reflect on challenges that face them, they engage the spiritual nature of their work as they direct their focus beyond routine issues or questions before them and seek to define their reason for being (mission) and the core values that they seek to uphold. On whose behalf does the organization exist? Mission and core values are touch points by which faith-based nonprofits infuse the Spirit into their work.

Boards do spiritual work when they transcend the physical with which they are surrounded and do generative work, when they look deep and seek to place the whole meeting under the guidance of the Spirit. Given the press of time, boards too often fail to ask such fundamental questions as "Why are we doing this?" "How do our values and our faith inform the way we make decisions?" If a board takes chasing the market and increasing the profit margin as its sole objective, it will in time lose its soul.

Many boards assess their effectiveness by how quickly they can move through their agendas. In this atmosphere, boards add little real value to what would happen without them. Boards deepen their contribution when they learn to wait on the Spirit and listen to each other. That takes time. It requires patience. But the results are better decisions.

Quaker boards practice a time of silence as a discipline to quiet their minds, to stop the noise of words, and wait on each other and the Spirit. This allows fresh insight to emerge.

We serve on boards that pause at strategic times for a time of silence and prayer. Some boards conclude their meetings with a time of reflection, asking, "How did we experience the movement of the Spirit in our work today?"

Finally, and perhaps most important, we remind ourselves that governing boards are composed of individuals. Experience bears evidence that the spiritual health and personal faith of the individual board members and staff have a significant influence on how decisions are made.

The meditations in this chapter are written by a wide variety of persons, drawing from many rich spiritual traditions. We hope these meditations will motivate board members, individually and collectively, to make spirituality a conscious part of their deliberations. (See graphic in part 1.) Incorporate spirituality into your value statement. Conduct your meetings with an awareness of God's presence, being reminded, as stated in the familiar Lord's Prayer, that the kingdom, the power, and the glory belong to God, forever and ever.

Select a meditation from this chapter that best speaks to the situation facing your board. Conclude your devotional time with a prayer from the end of the chapter, again feeling free to add to it and adapt it. Use silence and thoughtful pauses. Be relaxed and worshipful. The goal is to set a spiritual tone that will pervade the entire meeting.

Preparing to Meet

> So Christ himself gave the apostles, the prophets, the evangelists, the pastors and teachers, to equip his people for works of service, so that the body of Christ may be built up until we all reach unity in the faith and in the knowledge of the Son of God and become mature, attaining to the whole measure of the fullness of Christ.
> —Paul, in Ephesians 4:11-13 NIV

Boards often face significant decisions. At these moments, board members may become apprehensive. Uncertainty and difficult decisions can paralyze an entire board. But instead of paralysis, we must view these moments as opportunities to focus on what is positive within a difficult environment. In preparation for these challenges, we should purposely convene in ways that nurture our spirit, resulting in openness to engage and make decisions with optimism and hope, as promised in the Scripture quoted above.

Good boards are composed of complementary individuals and skill sets. These verses illustrate how faith-based boards come together, forming a larger body in the service of God. What a tremendous opportunity when boards summon the Spirit of God into these moments of significant deliberation! As part of the larger body, we must look out for each other, especially our spiritual pulse. We must seek the highest level of spiritual unity.

I seek to embrace the Spirit as I enter into board meetings. The biggest challenge is disengaging my bias and ego while engaging openness and alertness to the Spirit. How does one empty the mind of prejudices and become open to understanding the fullness of God?

Prayer as a centering practice is basic. Prayer soothes the heart and clears the mind. I continually ask for patience and vision. I need patience to allow issues to permeate my mind in spite of my biases and ego. I ask for vision to understand the larger community we serve, and I find that energizing. When facing difficult decisions, we do well to engage in centering prayer.

Focusing on what matters and on the people we serve is crucial. It is imperative that, as a board member, I can transport myself into the reality of the mission I am serving. Purposeful focus is required. Meeting three or four times a year makes it difficult to develop sharp focus. But that is the task we signed up for, and we must perform at our best if we are to help the people we serve through the entities we direct. Difficult decisions require extraordinary focus, and we must come prepared for such a task.

Preparation has many dimensions. One must engage with and understand the issues at hand. We must take extra care to prepare for board meetings; yet at moments of heightened difficulty, we need to make special efforts to grasp the issues at hand. We must also be self-aware of our limitations, thus relying on the Spirit and the rest of the board to enlighten each other. We must bring each other along in developing a more-complete understanding of the challenge being faced.

I consider it a successful board engagement if I leave a meeting feeling humbled by the opportunity of serving others, spiritually energized from experiencing God's presence, and fulfilled from offering my best.

—Jim Alvarez of Goshen, Indiana, is senior vice president of corporate services at Everence, a financial and mutual aid organization.

God Is in Our Midst

> For where two or three gather in my name, there am I
> with them.
>
> —Jesus, in Matthew 18:20 NIV

On my church office wall, I have a small print of Andrei Rublev's fifteenth-century painting titled *Trinity*. This remarkable painting depicts three divine angel-like beings seated around a table. Strangely the painting portrays an empty place front and center at the table, in the midst of the three angelic characters. These colorfully robed beings sit in a seamless equality of spirit with one another, each with a staff in hand, suggesting their role of care for those to whom they are sent.

Historically it was believed that the painting symbolized the Trinity as the three mysterious guests to whom Abraham and Sarah extended hospitality, as described in Genesis 18. Down through the years this painting has become an icon for religious people, a simple aid to focus their prayers and keep clear their calling as Christians. While icons have little place in the devotional life for many Protestant Christians, this particular icon has come to mean a great deal to me.

As our church board gathers for our monthly meeting, I hold in my memory Rublev's *Trinity*. We too gather around a table to be about the purposes of God for the congregation we lead. Instead of a staff in our hands, board members are more likely to have a laptop. While we don't make a point of keeping an empty place at the table, I like to visualize that our table includes an empty space where God is present and an active participant in our deliberations.

When we become bogged down in unhelpful discussion, this historic Russian icon calls me back to the promise of Jesus that "where two or three gather," he is in our midst. Even in those times when we are lost in our own thoughts or debating a hot topic, God is among us.

Writer Henri Nouwen suggests that Rublev was offering this icon as a means of keeping our hearts centered in God while living amid all kinds of unrest. It reminds us that our conversation as a board is about more than our human preoccupations. It offers a gentle invitation to open ourselves to the unseen divine Guest who provides wisdom and insight beyond our own capacities. That is my wish and prayer for the boards with which I serve.

Perhaps an icon doesn't convey that desire for everyone. An empty chair at the table, or the flame of a burning candle or lamp, or an open copy of the Scriptures—any of these can provide a reminder that the work will be incomplete without the presence of the Divine among us.

Sometimes the Scripture from Matthew 18 is used to console churchgoers when only a few people show up for a meeting. Instead of consolation, Jesus is offering a sturdy promise that when we gather in Jesus' name, we are not left to our own devices. We can meet in confidence that the God who calls us and gifts us will also provide for us all we need for effectiveness in doing God's work in the world.

As we gather for our board meetings, what reminds us that the work we do will only be fruitful if done in God's name? Is there a place at the table for a divine Guest? Is there space in the conversation to engage that presence in our dialogue? We can claim the promise of Jesus as we go about the meeting of our board.

—Miriam F. Book of Harleysville, Pennsylvania, is lead pastor of Salford Mennonite Church and board member of Goshen College and Living Branches.

Aware of God's Presence?

> Where can I go from your spirit? Or where can I flee from
> your presence?
> If I ascend to heaven, you are there; if I make my bed in
> Sheol, you are there.
> If I take the wings of the morning and settle at the farthest
> limits of the sea,
> even there your hand shall lead me, and your right hand shall
> hold me fast.
> If I say, "Surely the darkness shall cover me, and the light
> around me become night,"
> even the darkness is not dark to you;
> > the night is as bright as the day, for darkness is as light
> > > to you.
> > > > —Psalm 139:7-12

Soon after starting in business, my life became a whirlwind of activity. Days were filled: dealing with employee issues, attending meetings, solving problems, managing projects, and acquiring more education. I was building my career without even thinking about it. One position led to another so that in ten years my responsibilities probably exceeded what was warranted by my age and experience. Gradually the growing responsibilities included businesses nationally, layering travel on top of an already-busy schedule.

In parallel with the all-consuming business pursuits, I took on responsibilities within my local congregation: Sunday school teacher, deacon, church board member, and congregational chair. Congregational involvement led to denominational involvement, which meant even more travel. To this activity, I added involvement in a growing number of nonprofit organizations. By default, not design or plan, family was low in the pecking order of priorities. Familiar?

Exhausted, after twenty years of trying to keep up, I came to realize that all of this couldn't be held together. I had become a virtual agnostic: God was not a part of my daily life. I lived as if God did not exist. My life was controlled by the anxiety of schedule—always falling short. Out of desperation I was forced to "fit God in" or risk losing it.

So I began each morning with a brief time of quiet prayer and solitude. Ever so slowly I started to see God's presence, almost like footprints, in the events and interactions of my day. God became a reality, not a concept. God's presence was real and relevant. What was out of order slowly began to take on a new sense of order.

I discovered that God is always present with me. So I ask myself, "Am I present with God? Can we be present with God?"

What would happen if each board member, individually and collectively, would make an effort to be present with God? How would we make decisions? How would we face the challenges that confront us? How would we react to success? To failure? What would change if in our hearts we were more conscious of God at work in our midst? If we paused to seek divine direction in our work and planning? What if the unseen God became as real as what we see? Can our meetings be soaked in God's presence? It can happen only if we are deliberately present with God.

John's Gospel pictures the Spirit as a wind. Can we think of the Spirit as the wind of God, gently filling the room in which we meet?

Mother Teresa said: "God is everywhere and in everything, and we are all his children. God is everywhere and in everything, and without him we cannot exist. When we gather in his name, this gives us strength."

—R. Lee Delp of Lansdale, Pennsylvania, is a boardroom veteran with profit and nonprofit organizations.

The Spirituality of Work

> Whatever you do, do it all for the glory of God.
> —Paul, in 1 Corinthians 10:31b NIV

At the end of a sociology course several years ago, a student commented that she wished it had been more spiritual. I told her that we were using the intellect that God had given us to learn more about God's world. I reminded her that I had started the class with a meditation in which I proposed that we were learning sociology so we could be part of the answer to the Lord's Prayer: "Your will be done, on earth as it is in heaven." When I asked her what "more spiritual" would look like, she said we should have a devotional meditation and prayer at the beginning of each class. I assured her that I do pray regularly about the class and that many students do too, particularly on test days.

This student linked spirituality with a set of spiritual symbols and acts that spread a spiritual veneer over the day-to-day tasks rather than seeing the work itself as spiritual. As a child, I remember thinking that I would not have had to wash dishes, dust, or mow the lawn if Adam and Eve had behaved themselves: I regarded work as punishment.

Many of my students frame a Christian perspective on work as chiefly meaning extras such as witnessing to colleagues and not going to office parties where inappropriate things are done. We can develop a sacred and secular dichotomy in which we treat work as secular and limit the impact of the spiritual to an overlay of spiritual piety. To be sure, shared spiritual rituals and symbols are necessary. However, an understanding of the spirituality of work will recognize that work is part of God's design for the world. It will both elevate work to the status that God wants and help us come closer to God through work.

Pope John Paul II in his encyclical on Human Work (*Laborem Exercens*, 1991) links our work to God's work in the world and calls for the awareness that our work is participation in God's activity to permeate even the most ordinary and everyday activities. According to Dorothy Sayers, the first demand that a carpenter's "religion makes upon him is that he should make good tables."[1]

Part of seeing work as a spiritual activity is the understanding that when done to the glory of God, it is as spiritual as prayer and singing praise and worship songs. It is a challenge to transcend the dichotomy that divides things into sacred and secular categories. What the student failed to see was that in our intellectual and creative work, we reflect our creation in the image of God. Yet not all work is sacred. Some is dehumanizing both in the way it is done and in its effects on other people and the world.

Work, even menial and mundane toil, is in and of itself spiritual when it is done to the glory of God and is part of God's activity in the world to make life rich and abundant.

—John W. Eby of Dillsburg, Pennsylvania, is professor of sociology at Messiah College and board chair of Landis Homes, a retirement community near Lititz, Pennsylvania.

Speak the Truth in Love and Humility

> Beware of the yeast of the Pharisees, that is, their hypocrisy.
> Nothing is covered up that will not be uncovered, and noth-
> ing secret that will not become known.
>
> —Jesus, in Luke 12:1-2

We meet around our board table as a chosen few. Because we are committed to the mission, and because we give freely to put the mission into action, we have been selected to join this elite circle. No, it isn't a cushy assignment; it's more work and added responsibility, all without remuneration. But even the acknowledgment of this additional burden is a compliment: we are here because we are strong enough to carry the extra load.

And so, as our leader guides us through the day's agenda, we carry this identity: the strong, the good, the elect.

It's a setup, really. We didn't audition to be special, and truth be told, we often don't feel very special. But here we are, trustees together of a good and noble cause. It puts us on our best behavior, and we are determined never to let down the team by being negative or discordant. And so, when our leader asks us about the charitable giving goal, the letter-writing campaign, or the proposal to launch a new program, we respond reflexively with the appropriate answer.

And what is the appropriate answer? Isn't it usually the answer one would expect, given our identity as the strong, the good, and the elect?

When Jesus warned his disciples about the Pharisees, he described their hypocrisy as "yeast." It was the active element, the energy that made them a force to be reckoned with. Because they were reputed to occupy the ethical high ground—speaking for God, as it were—the Pharisees were the yardstick against which others measured themselves. This was the source of their authority: no one wanted to fail to measure up.

But high standards not tempered by candor and humility quickly evolve into pretense and lies, blocking the light and the path forward. That's what happened to the Pharisees, and it is why Jesus issued his warning. Those who see themselves as righteous guardians can easily become incapable of being honest about how things really are. Despite good intentions, they become blind guides.

As board members, the lesson is not to care less about doing good. It is not to hold our roles as directors in less respect. Instead, the lesson is to recognize how easily our highest values and aspirations can become a pious cant, mere lip service that reflects well on us but has little connection to the reality of life. The lesson is to take this danger seriously and to liberally season our lofty aspirations with candor and humility. That will keep us open to the light and the path forward.

So how are things, really? Let us together affirm that it is appropriate to describe things as they are, or as we see them—no pretense! How might we make them better? What affirmations and reservations do we have about what is being proposed? Suggestions for improvement are always welcome in a healthy organization.

Uncovering "the secret things" may seem to be a threat. Can we instead simply hear such thoughts as a counsel of realism? As best we know it, we speak the truth to one another in love and humility. We get it out in the open and then bring our values and aspirations to bear upon it. This is how we find our way to the light, as God is our help.

—Berry Friesen of Lancaster, Pennsylvania, is an attorney who has served on several nonprofit boards and was executive director of the Pennsylvania Hunger Action Center, Harrisburg.

Pray out of Your Lives

> [Jesus] was praying in a certain place, and after he had finished, one of his disciples said to him, "Lord, teach us to pray, as John taught his disciples." He said to them, "When you pray, say:
>
> Father, hallowed be your name.
>
> Your kingdom come.
>
> Give us each day our daily bread.
>
> And forgive us our sins, for we ourselves forgive everyone indebted to us.
>
> And do not bring us to the time of trial."
>
> —Luke 11:1-4

Learning to pray is a lifelong task for most of us. Learning how to pray in the boardroom has its own particular challenges. Many boards set aside time for opening devotions when they gather. Often the members share a blessing before meals, and some sessions end with prayers of sending. All those prayer forms can play important roles in the lifework of a board. But it is also possible for standard prayer times to become pro forma.

It wasn't dry ritual that we faced when the Mennonite World Conference executive committee met annually, however. Most of our committee members were champion prayers, well practiced in the art of holding up their communities before God and making space for God's Spirit to work among them. Rather, ours was the challenge of becoming a real, functioning body. Meeting only once a year meant that we needed to become reacquainted every time we gathered. In addition, we brought several different first languages to the table, as well as a bewildering variety of family, church, socioeconomic, and political circumstances.

In response to our needs, we practiced using our entire first meeting session to hear from each other and to collect the causes for prayer that we brought to the meeting. We made a long list of requests and thanksgivings on a white board: a husband's concerns for the surgery his wife was facing, a father's hopes for the marriage of a daughter, a bishop's struggles with how to respond to the cost of living in a country where inflation was spiraling out of control, a pastor's dreams for the survival and thriving of her small rural congregation, and the struggles of a church in a country wracked by violence.

Then, throughout our meeting, we set aside time for evening prayers. We sang and read Scripture together, and different members of the committee took leadership in raising several of our specific requests in prayer. Those prayer times, as well as the emerging energy that came from diving into our agenda, helped to hold our committee together and remind us of our reason for being there.

When Luke tells the story of Jesus, he underlines over and over that Jesus was a man of prayer. From his first appearance as an adult in Luke's Gospel (3:21), Jesus prayed. Prayer was also part of the life of his predecessor John the Baptist, and eventually his disciples caught on. But they recognized that prayer was not something that one just did. Rather, the disciples needed to learn *how*. Jesus responded with the words familiar to us as the Lord's Prayer. When we take a new look at these words, we see that they carefully include the most daily of needs: "bread"; political realities: "*your* kingdom come"; and relationships within the community: "for we ourselves forgive everyone."

Most boards don't have as much time in each meeting as did our international body. But finding ways to weave the prayers of our lives and the places we come from into the warp and woof of the meeting allowed God's presence to invigorate all our discussions and even to shape our decisions.

—Nancy R. Heisey of Harrisonburg, Virginia, is undergraduate academic dean at Eastern Mennonite University and was moderator of Mennonite World Conference in 2003–9.

A Position of Power

> Then Jesus came to them and said, "All authority in heaven
> and on earth has been given to me. Therefore go and make
> disciples of all nations, baptizing them in the name of the
> Father and of the Son and of the Holy Spirit, and teaching
> them to obey everything I have commanded you. And surely
> I am with you always, to the very end of the age."
> —Matthew 28:18-20 NIV

While attending a reunion of Mennonite Central Committee
Southern Africa workers, some friends and I were catching up on
what had happened to us over the past 25 years. I was at the time
executive director of a faith-based retirement community that had
435 units for elderly persons at various stages of independence. My
friends asked about the details of my work. Among other things,
I told them that I had just finished reading the Gospels through
the "eyes of an administrator." Their immediate response was "But
you are in a position of power."

The comment both surprised and perplexed me. I made a few
other remarks. The response was the same: "You are in a position of
power." The "position of power" did not sit well with them. They
seemed to be uncomfortable with and even suspicion of someone
being "in a position of power." As an out, I changed the topic to
something that could make us all comfortable.

The conversation, however, stayed with me. Why is leadership, and the power and authority associated with it, looked
upon with suspicion and mistrust?

I don't ever recall thinking, "Someday I want to be an executive director with power and authority." My career in healthcare
just somehow evolved. I began as a staff nurse. In that position
I had the power and authority to do what a staff nurse does. As
other opportunities presented themselves, I was given the power
and authority to do that particular job. As executive director I was
also given power and authority to do my job. All the other staff
in the organization also had power and authority to do their jobs.

I choose to read the Gospels because my organization was
embarking on a major expansion and renovation project. This

would bring about many changes. The changes were actually good changes. However, change is change. And change makes staff nervous. I needed a model. I thought that observing Jesus' interactions—with people who had needs and with those who had opinions on how things should be done—would be a good start. Jesus' use of parables was especially inspiring. I found myself using short stories as introductions to some of issues with which we were dealing.

Some Gospel passages made me chuckle. The Matthew 28:18-20 passage quoted above was one such passage. I know it has been used frequently as "a call to missions." It asks for soul-searching, sacrifice, and commitment. Why did this passage give me a chuckle? It seems so simple, so textbook perfect.

- Mission and vision: making disciples—clear, concise *direction*
- Job description: baptize and teach—clear, concise *responsibility*
- Skills: everything I have commanded you—clear, concise *training*
- Support: I will be with you always—clear, concise *empowerment*

We do have power and authority to be focused, to take on responsibility, to develop our skills, and to empower others. Power and authority to serve.

—Herta Janzen of Winnipeg, Manitoba, has served as executive director of Donwood Manor and is a board member of the Winnipeg Regional Health Authority.

Daniel's Leadership

> Now Daniel so distinguished himself among the adminis-
> trators and the satraps by his exceptional qualities that the
> king planned to set him over the whole kingdom. At this,
> the administrators and the satraps tried to find grounds
> for charges against Daniel in his conduct of government
> affairs, but they were unable to do so. They could find no
> corruption in him, because he was trustworthy and neither
> corrupt nor negligent.
>
> —Daniel 6:3-4 NIV

I have served on nonprofit boards that were confronted with difficult decisions, even questions of continuation: hard choices needed to be made, including cutting staff, limiting services, or risking a new initiative. These decisions result in anxiety and sleeplessness.

During these times I remind myself of the example of Daniel. He was a great leader because he was a person of integrity, reliability, and prayer.

In his book *The Speed of Trust*, Stephen Covey writes that building trust is key to success in an organization. It speeds up and increases accomplishments. Covey identifies two key components of building trust: integrity and competence.[2]

Integrity means to be above reproach. Daniel was honest and without corruption. As hard as his enemies tried, they could find absolutely no fault in him. Even though the ruler of the land allowed Daniel to rise quickly to the top of the political heap, Daniel didn't give in to pride or to the temptation of being self-serving. He continued to make personal integrity a priority. In 1 Timothy 3:1-2 we read: "Here is a trustworthy saying: If anyone sets his heart on being an overseer, he desires a noble task. Now the overseer *must be above reproach*" (emphasis added). A life of integrity can serve as protection against false accusation, as Psalm 25:21 says: "May integrity and uprightness protect me, because my hope is in you."

Daniel was also reliable and capable. He followed through on his word. Over time, he gained people's trust by making sure that his actions were consistent with his words. His "yes" was "yes," and his "no" was "no." He always did what he said he would do. People with whom he worked and lived had learned that they could count on him.

In addition, Daniel prayed for wisdom in his leadership role, and he boldly prayed for his people. He looked to God daily for guidance in his difficult task as a leader. He recognized the weight of his responsibility and his need for God's sustenance.

Daniel's example encourages leaders to be trustworthy, competent, and reliable; to follow through on their word, as persons of honesty and integrity. It encourages leaders to pray daily for wisdom, a clear vision, and faithfulness to their mission. As time goes on, all who support our organization will come to rely on us to fulfill the responsibilities that God has placed in our hands.

—Ruth Keidel Clemens, Baltimore, Maryland, serves as executive director, Mennonite Central Committee East Coast.

Making Space for Spiritual Direction

> Yet among the mature we do speak wisdom, though it
> is not a wisdom of this age or of the rulers of this age,
> who are doomed to perish. But we speak God's wisdom,
> secret and hidden, which God decreed before the ages for
> our glory. . . . And we speak of these things in words not
> taught by human wisdom but taught by the Spirit, inter-
> preting spiritual things to those who are spiritual.
> —Paul, in 1 Corinthians 2:6-7, 13

> Spiritual direction is, in reality, nothing more than a way
> of leading us to see and obey the real Director—the Holy
> Spirit hidden in the depths of our soul.
> —Thomas Merton, Trappist monk

Many of us are privileged to work with a spiritual director, seeking to better understand God's hand on our life journey. Spiritual directors ask questions that encourage us to open our eyes and truly see what God is doing in our life. Have you ever invited a spiritual director to be part of a large group meeting, to help the group take notice of God at work in the midst of the conversation?

Mennonite Central Committee, as it approached its 90th anniversary, engaged in an extensive revisioning and restructuring process. It involved 60 meetings with over 2,000 people from 50 countries participating. A leadership group of 30 people absorbed all this information and, in a final summit of 100 people, met for several days to wrestle together with discerning God's call for us. Spiritual directors were invited to walk with us in all these meetings, to give emphasis to God's presence—with the freedom to interrupt the leaders and the process at any time.

Each spiritual director brought a completely different style, and each had a profound impact on the group discussion. One brought images to fill the room, bringing us face-to-face with God visually. One brought questions, only questions, disturbing questions. One brought his own story of encountering God. All brought us to conscious thought of opening ourselves to the leading of the Spirit, to God's presence amid debate and discernment.

This was a new experience for most of the participants. It was also rather uncomfortable for many. It differed from the more-familiar spoken prayers at the beginning and the end of a meeting. All the images, questions, and stories were disturbing rather than reassuring. As the meeting organizer, I was worried that the experience might be so unsettling as to distort the outcome. I had given these spiritual directors freedom to interfere and intervene, and when they did, I worried a lot! They knew little about our topics or issues or controversies, and yet each of them stepped right into the debate and led us in spiritual discernment. In the end, they were a gift to us. But I had to work hard at trusting them and the process.

We normally begin and end meetings with prayer. We work on an attitude of openness to the leading of God's Spirit. And yet, sometimes we need more. Boards need to invite someone to be their spiritual director, either from within their ranks or from the outside. To interrupt and intervene. To ask questions that may be troubling to some. To lead us to ponder together on what God is saying. Not necessarily to say a spoken prayer, but to guide us toward God.

Is there a spiritual director in our group today, informally or explicitly? Are we ready to listen, to hear God, and to be distracted from our agenda, to be brought into tune with God's agenda? Are we prepared to give someone the authority to do this in our meeting? Can we make space for spiritual direction in our corporate life as well as our personal lives?

God is present with us, but sometimes we need spiritual leadership to experience that presence consciously and act on it.

—Arli Klassen of Lancaster, Pennsylvania, serves as executive director of Mennonite Central Committee in Akron, Pennsylvania.

Little Prayers

> Seven times a day I praise you.
> —Psalm 119:164 NIV

"You need the little prayers," William Rutherford told us in a retreat in Northern Ireland. Rutherford, a retired Irish minister, was introducing our group of pilgrims to the prayer practices of ancient Celtic Christians.

My heart immediately warmed as Rutherford spoke because it had been the "little prayers" of Celtic Christians that had first attracted me to Celtic spirituality. As I came across them in my reading, I claimed them and found myself praying them often, little prayers like "I on your path, O God; You, O God, on my way."

Celtic Christians prayed this prayer at the beginning of a journey, both as a way of remembering God's presence near at hand, and also as a commitment to walk with God. It didn't matter whether the journey was as short as walking to a nearby field to tend sheep, or as long as a journey across the sea to another coast.

One day in a class I taught on prayer, we were discussing the prayers we had learned as children, especially prayers for the beginning and end of the day. A student from Northern Ireland raised her hand and repeated a prayer that she had prayed every morning:

> Thanks be to you, O God, that I have risen this day
> to the rising of this life itself.
> May it be a day of blessing, O God, of every gift,
> a day of new beginnings given.
> Help me to avoid every sin and the source of every sin to
> forsake.
> And as the mist scatters from the crest of the hills,
> may each ill haze clear from my soul, O God.

Having grown up in Oregon, where mornings are often moist and misty, the vivid image of sin evaporating from my life as the morning sun breaks through the clouds immediately captured my attention. With its simple beauty and rhythm, this morning prayer was easy to memorize, and I soon claimed it as my own.

My interest in these prayers led me to take a course in Celtic spirituality and then to visit ancient Celtic sites in the British Isles. Eventually I planned and led pilgrimages, such as the one described above. People could discover the riches of this spiritual tradition of prayers offered throughout the day, prayers in which God seems very near.

I learned that Celtic Christians had prayers for making a fire in the morning, milking cows, baking bread, or churning butter. They offered prayers before sowing seed in their fields or gathering the harvest. With such "little prayers," each moment and relationship could be filled with a sense of Christ's intimate presence. Resources are available in J. Philip Newell's *Celtic Prayers from Iona* or in his *Celtic Benediction: Morning and Night Prayer.*[3]

Prayer practices like these were not unique to Celtic Christians: the practice of pausing to pray throughout the day is common to many religious traditions. One psalm speaks of praising God "seven times a day" (Ps 119:164); the first Christians gathered to pray together at dawn and at nightfall. Throughout the centuries, monastic communities have paused at set times throughout the day and night to offer praise to God and to intercede for the world. In each of these traditions, the animating desire has been to nurture a continual awareness of God's presence and call amid daily life.

The special gift of the Celtic tradition is one that is much needed in our time, especially on days when we are busy with meetings and crowded agendas. In a world that often forgets God's presence, we too can pause even while a meeting is in process to remember our Creator, to be filled again with the love of Christ, and to open ourselves to the Spirit's guidance.

—Marlene Kropf is associate professor of spiritual formation and worship, Associated Mennonite Biblical Seminary, and the former denominational minister of worship for Mennonite Church USA.

How Do You Prepare to Meet?

The human mind may devise many plans,
  but it is the purpose of the LORD that will be established.
                              —Proverbs 19:21

For eight years I served as the executive secretary for a denominational leadership board that met for three days twice a year. Needless to say, with meetings so infrequent and for so long at a time, our agenda became quite intense. People flew to the meetings from all across North America and Puerto Rico. For days our small staff was busily working at the agenda and making all the hosting arrangements. Who will provide shuttle service to and from the airport? How do we plan for the meals? Will board members sleep in a hotel or be hosted in homes of church members? Planning for meetings of the board became high drama.

This was before email and the Internet: to each board member we mailed a huge docket with the agenda and supporting materials. The expectation was that each member would read the materials well in advance of the meeting and come prepared to actively engage the items for action in our board sessions.

But how would I as their executive officer prepare for the meeting? I invested considerable time in preparing the agenda, and I was reasonably apprised of the issues for which decisions needed to be made. While other people attended to logistics, how should I prepare for my role in these demanding board sessions?

More than once I took my large docket—even bigger than the version sent to the board members—and retreated to a wooded center, where I reserved space at a place called The Hut for a day of quiet. Much of the day was spent in praying through the agenda. In most cases I knew the direction I hoped the board would take—but what direction did God want us to take? The information for discussion and decision making was on paper. But were my heart and my spirit attuned to God? Was I prepared to release this packet of information, recommendations, and statistics to God's Spirit for guidance?

Sometimes that day in The Hut went quickly. Sometimes I became bogged down in details that distracted me from the purpose of the day. But I always left glad that I had taken the time out of an otherwise busy schedule to move from logistics and reports to my own spiritual preparation.

I am convinced that how we prepare ourselves for a board meeting is as important as the materials we assemble for board consideration. I need to let go and know that if this work is truly of God, then God must be in the center of our board deliberations. Beyond the specific agenda items is a mission and a purpose greater than us, and we will only complete this mission through prayerful preparation for our work together as a board.

How do we prepare for our meetings of the board? Have we prayed through the agenda and prepared ourselves for the hard work of board deliberations? The results of the meeting require not only good information sharing, but also good listening to the voice of God within and through one another.

—James Lapp is preaching pastor of Salford Mennonite Church and vice chair of the Bridge of Hope board.

Attentive to the Light

> Your word is a lamp to my feet
> and a light to my path.
>
> —Psalm 119:105

A few years ago our congregation called a new church board to leadership. After a season of stress and tension around previous boards, it was important that the new board begin with spiritual centeredness and strength. So on the Sunday when the new board was commissioned, we pastors gave the board chair a ceramic oil lamp with the words "Let this lamp burn brightly in the center of each meeting of the board as a symbol of the light of God's Spirit among you. Allow the lamp to remind you that Jesus, the Light of the World, is in your midst as you lead our congregation."

Now, in each meeting of the board, the lamp is lit and burns throughout the meeting. But this same lamp shows up on various other occasions in the life of the congregation: at the Ash Wednesday service, on the table for the Good Friday service, or whenever we need a reminder that apart from God's light we flounder in darkness.

Like so many other tasks in life, the work of a church board can become just that: "work" at one more assignment in the context of our busy lives. In spite of our claim to be servants of Jesus, our gathering around the table with agenda before us can soon degenerate into a churchly version of one of the myriad boards that dutifully assemble once a month in our community.

The Scriptures assure us that God's word provides the needed light for us personally and for us as leaders in our organizational responsibilities. Working on the budget may not feel very spiritual. The lamp reminds us that our finances must reflect a mission and vision greater than the numbers on the page. The daunting challenges of technology changing faster than we can either understand or afford can be overwhelming. Might we need a reminder that our work depends more on the radiance of God's light than the latest gadgetry we might purchase?

I have just received the board packet for the next meeting of a nonprofit on which I serve. The staff does excellent work in assembling the information that the board needs for fruitful sessions together. In our meeting we will be asked to discuss and discern some new options that could drastically impact the future of the organization. Where and how do we receive the wisdom needed when the very viability of the organization seems to be at stake? That is precisely when we need the lamp to remind us of the availability of God's light for such decisions.

What rituals remind your board that the work you do together is really ministry in the name of Jesus? What reminds us that our work has significance exceeding the current fiscal year, maybe stretching into eternity?

I wish I could say that something as simple as an oil lamp can make every meeting exciting. It's a symbol, and the greater reality is the light of our Lord that it represents. Finally, it's that presence of which the lamp is a gentle reminder that makes all the difference.

—James Lapp is preaching pastor of Salford Mennonite Church and vice chair of the Bridge of Hope board.

Meetings as Worship?

> Beloved, I do not consider that I have made it my own; but this one thing I do: forgetting what lies behind and straining forward to what lies ahead, I press on toward the goal for the prize of the heavenly call of God in Christ Jesus. Let those of us then who are mature be of the same mind; and if you think differently about anything, this too God will reveal to you. Only let us hold fast to what we have attained.
>
> —Paul, in Philippians 3:13-16

> Wisdom is knowing what to do next,
> Skill is knowing how to do it,
> and Virtue is doing it!
>
> —David Starr Jordan[4]

The tone of most of our meetings is set by the devotion or meditation that precedes getting into the heart of the meeting. There is usually some fleshing out of the agenda, and finally, boldly or timidly, we arrive at the heart of the meeting. When I come committed to being guided by God, I pray for the agenda, for each participant, and for those who made the preparations for the meeting. My prayer is that we will come together with like minds, to achieve our vision. The meeting agenda is already at the goal line, waiting for us to catch up.

I am reminded of the early days of my service, when I was positive that I did not know enough about church doctrine to serve in the capacity to which I was elected. After work I read and reread the dockets until it was time to go to a meeting. I was always frantic that I had not covered all the materials or made enough notes along the margins of the pages. It bothered me, and I decided that I needed to feel more secure. That is when I started to pray over every page and to write little prayers in the margins of the pages. I went from one-line prayers to prayers that lapped into the text of the page. These prayers led to greater confidence and joy and satisfaction in serving and leading. It was as if I could see God's hand in the development of my commitment and service to the church.

Then with that practice, I came to the realization that when I acknowledge that God is in control, I can sit back and watch God's hand move to encompass the growing church and the growing community.

I often thought that I had to set the right tone and atmosphere for my meetings. I came to understand that God in the meeting transforms the meeting. God brings truth, richness of energy, spontaneity of ideas, solutions, and—the goal line.

I was led to pray that God would light up the small duties of this life to shine with the beauty of God's countenance. I came to see that joy dwells in the commonest of tasks. I was reminded that we do all for the sake of Jesus Christ our Lord, in whose name we pray and serve. Thus we are "forgetting what lies behind and straining forward to what lies ahead" (Phil 3:13).

—Ivorie Lowe of Markham, Illinois, has been a school administrator and served on the boards of Mennonite Church USA and Goshen College.

The Power of Silence

A fundamental principle of the Religious Society of Friends is the belief that my faith, my relationship with God, and my experience with how God's presence is revealed in my life—all this is mine, and mine alone. To quote Janet Shepherd, a Quaker historian and teacher: "This is how it is for me." This writing is offered as my experience in working to be more conscious of God's Spirit in board service and leadership.

Organizations with their roots in the unprogrammed tradition of the Religious Society of Friends (Quakers) usually begin their meetings with a period of silence. This silence is rooted in the belief that a decision or path forward will become apparent when we conduct our business with openness to the leadings of the Spirit. The silence is an opportunity to clear our heads, detach from the distractions around us and the tension and pace of the world, and open our minds to the possibilities that may emerge.

Sometimes the silence is peaceful and still, like the mirror-smooth surface of a lake on a calm day. And sometimes the silence is deafening, so full of thoughts and sounds and ideas that it does not seem like silence at all. That is when I need more—more silence, more calm, more openness.

The principle of openness requires that participants approach the meeting with an open mind, without a preconceived notion of how things should evolve or be resolved, without a personal agenda to advance. Yet we have an expectation that we will discover the right way to move forward. We trust that as we listen to those present bringing their gifts and wisdom to the process and allow ourselves to be open to the possibilities and the guidance of God, we will find our way. Our belief in continuing revelation, that the truth we know now may not be the truth of tomorrow, calls us to be open and receptive as we conduct our business. And when the path forward becomes apparent, we will know and we will feel the calm and serenity of making a decision that is right. This requires careful attention to the subtle movements of the Spirit.

When a board is facing a difficult decision or there is conflict among members, the silence and openness are more important than ever. Sometimes the "noise" of conflict or dissonance is deafening in the silence. As a leader, I have to work hard to quiet the cacophony and ask God for his wisdom to lead in a way that reflects his will, to be open to hearing his guidance and Spirit at work. Times such as these can feel as though we are carrying the weight of the world, yet when I am truly open to the process and trust that the right path will become apparent, it is as if the weight is lifted. The way forward is clear, and the silence is peaceful and still.

—Jane Mack of Gwynedd, Pennsylvania, is executive director of Friends Services for the Aging.

The Holy Work of Budget

> When it grew late, his disciples came to him and said,
> "This is a deserted place, and the hour is now very late;
> send them away so that they may go into the surrounding
> country and villages and buy something for themselves to
> eat." . . . And he said to them, "How many loaves have
> you? Go and see." When they had found out, they said,
> "Five, and two fish." Then he ordered them to get all the
> people to sit down in groups on the green grass. So they
> sat down in groups of hundreds and of fifties. Taking the
> five loaves and the two fish, he looked up to heaven, and
> blessed and broke the loaves, and gave them to his dis-
> ciples to set before the people; and he divided the two fish
> among them all. And all ate and were filled.
> —Mark 6:35-42

We were knee-deep in the budget process. The work was overdue, and there were last-minute manipulations taking place as we tried to make the dollars work. We knew that this should be holy work, work that captured our highest hopes and dreams for who we want to be, where we want to take our ministries. But this year, once again, it felt anything but holy or sacred. It felt secular, calculated, and sterile. Our focus was on numbers and metrics, on ratios and bond covenants. It seemed far from the care that defines us, removed from the needs we strive to meet daily, and detached from the faces of those we serve in the name of our loving God. How could this be?

The parable of the loaves and fishes is a two-part story. In it, Christ took basic resources and distributed them among the hungry. Though we commonly say he "multiplied" the loaves and fishes, this word is not found in any of the five Gospel accounts. Perhaps over time and across cultures and languages, we've added the concept that Christ multiplied the limited food at hand so that we could wrap our brains around it. Somehow we filled in that detail because it made sense to us, for after all, you can't feed a multitude on a few loaves and fishes. Or can you?

The other part of the story is equally important: "They all ate and were satisfied" (Mark 6:42 NIV). Nowhere does the Scripture tell us that everyone ate until they were full. It says simply that Jesus blessed the limited food, distributed it among the people, they ate and were satisfied. And there were leftovers to share on another day. All were satisfied, not only by the loaves and fishes, but also by the Word and the community they shared on that distant hillside.

Perhaps we can take the story of the loaves and fishes with us as we approach our budgets and the management of our ministries, especially in times that are financially trying. After all, they *are* about our highest hopes and dreams, and our commitment to advance God's mission. We have learned that in some years, budgets and management are about growth and new ideas, and in other years they are about satisfying the basics with a few loaves, fishes, and a community that shares. When we remember this and look at the abundance of resources we actually have before us, it is amazing how far those resources stretch, especially when we remember, as Christ did, to bless them as we distribute them across the multitude.

> Help us, gracious God, to remember your stories as we set about the sacred work of budgets. In your goodness help us see the resources we have, even when they seem to be too small to satisfy us. Teach us first to see our loaves and fishes for the abundance that they are; help us remember to bless them for your work and then to distribute them wisely. Show us what we can live without so that we can let go of those things gracefully. Grant us the wisdom to discern what we can't live without so that the essence of your presence lives always in our work. Help us to be as satisfied as the multitude on the hill was so many centuries ago. We pray this in your name. Amen.

—Peggy Mullan of Phoenix, Arizona, is president and CEO of Beatitudes Campus.

Relationships: Key to Effective Board Service

The Lord God said, "It is not good for the man to be alone."
—Genesis 2:18 NIV

Sometimes as I prepare for a board meeting, I reflect about the people with whom I am serving. What are their backgrounds? Their vocations? Are they married? With children? Grandchildren? The answers to these questions are largely factual. I know the answers or will shortly learn them. Our service together will allow us to become better acquainted. We will come to know each other's family backgrounds, vocations, marital and family status. We will learn the facts, but will we invest the time to really know them as people—their hopes, dreams, motivations, and values?

Jesus was a master at getting acquainted with the people with whom he associated. In the story of the "rich young ruler," Jesus was clearly dealing with a leader. This young leader came to Jesus with a fundamental question (Matt 19:16): "Teacher, what good thing must I do to have eternal life?" This is a question that most persons ask or at least think about. And Jesus knew the answer. What a wonderful opportunity for Jesus to bring another soul into the kingdom! As I read this story, I find myself almost saying, "Tell him, Jesus, tell him!"

But rather than retorting with an immediate answer, Jesus answered a question with a question: "Why do you ask me about what is good?" Jesus, we can postulate, wanted to start a conversation. Conversations are gateways to relationships, and relationship is what both Jesus and the young leader were seeking.

So it is with our fellow board members. They seek meaningful relationships. We were made for relationships. God created us as relational beings (Gen 2:18).

God desires to communicate with us through prayer, Scripture, meditation, and nature. But God most commonly communicates through people whom God has intentionally placed into our lives.

I was chairing a search committee for a new executive director of an influential community organization. As one of our three final candidates entered the room, it was clear to everyone that she was quite anxious. Her responses were tentative. Ten minutes into the interview, she admitted that she was extremely nervous and fearful that she was not interviewing well.

After she left the room, some committee members were minded to eliminate her from consideration. Then one member said, "She did not interview well, but what did you *feel*?" Slowly, one after another, we admitted that beyond the nervousness and stumbling answers, she appeared to be a warm, caring, highly relational person. We reminded ourselves that our intent was to hire a relationship builder, someone who would truly care about and connect with the people we were seeking to serve. We hired her, and the organization has flourished under her leadership.

If you were asked, "Why do you serve with the organizations you serve?" you are not likely to respond, "To build strong relationships." But in the absence of relationship building, organizations wither. Conversely, where relationships flourish, organizations flourish as well.

How well do you know your fellow board members? What would it take to begin building a deeper relationship today? What could your board accomplish if all members truly believed that God's primary means of communicating with you is through the person sitting next to you?

—Roger S. North of Lancaster, Pennsylvania, is founder and president of North Group Consultants; he also serves on numerous nonprofit boards.

In the Manner and Spirit of Jesus

> By contrast, the fruit of the Spirit is love, joy, peace,
> patience, kindness, generosity, faithfulness, gentleness,
> and self-control. There is no law against such things.
> —Paul, in Galatians 5:22-23

At one meeting of the Ontario Mennonite Youth Fellowship, I observed a board member red-faced and angry during a heated exchange. As the group's president, I agreed with his point of view but was troubled by the way he engaged in the discussion.

Another time I was in a phone conversation with a friend, making a point that was important to me. My wife overheard my side of the conversation and reflected that I seemed frustrated and angry.

As good as the intentions may have been in these two examples, they were not a demonstration of the fruit of God's Spirit, including gentleness.

My son and I interviewed sixty-one Mennonite Church leaders in North America for a Mennonite Church Canada-sponsored project called The Board and Staff Relationship in Christian Organizations. These leaders had served in 271 positions: 180 positions as volunteer board members and 91 staff positions, in more than 80 Mennonite Church and related organizations. An underlying assumption of the project was that if the board and staff relationship is healthy, we can better discern what God intends for the organization.

One of the questions was "What is the appropriate use of spiritual disciplines in building healthy board and staff relationships?" The responses indicated that spiritual disciplines build board and staff relationships. This is done in a group setting through personal sharing, prayer, Scripture, worship, and reflection. The benefits of corporate spiritual disciplines are that they help set the context and ground the group, with God as the center and we as stewards. By using spiritual disciplines in board and staff processes, we are led to ask what the Spirit is saying to us when the organization is faced with difficulty. This can, in turn, assist with the discernment of organizational vision.

These leaders linked spiritual disciplines closely with building board and staff relationships. Responses suggested that exercising these disciplines is the right and good thing to do and is beneficial for the organization. They saw a need to increase corporate prayer, Scripture reading, and worship as an integral part of the board and staff functioning. A few leaders cautioned that spiritual disciplines must not be used to control or manipulate others in the discernment process.

Jesus established the church as his body, to carry on his redemptive work in the world. Our ministries are part of the work of the church. As corporate members of this body of Christ, we carry on the work of Christ in the manner and spirit of Jesus: with "love, joy, peace, patience, kindness, generosity, faithfulness, gentleness, and self-control" (Gal 5:22-23).

You may consider incorporating the following statement, drawn from our work with organizations, into the core values of your ministry:

> We will integrate into the life of our board and staff functions the practice of corporate spiritual disciplines of prayer, Scripture, worship, and personal sharing, so as to build relationships that enable us to better discern God's intent for our organization. We will be vigilant that spiritual disciplines will not be misused in the decision-making processes.

—Andrew Reesor-McDowell of Markham, Ontario, works in children's mental health and is moderator of Mennonite Church Canada. Written with his son Allan Reesor-McDowell, who works for Mennonite Central Committee (Ontario).

Another Way of Seeing

> If the whole body were an eye, where would the sense of hearing be? If the whole body were an ear, where would the sense of smell be? But in fact God has arranged the parts in the body, every one of them, just as he wanted them to be. If they were all one part, where would the body be? As it is, there are many parts, but one body.
> —Paul, in 1 Corinthians 12:17-20 NIV

One of the defining characteristics of modern society is the way it has perfected organization. When people feel inconvenienced, they decry structure and organization. But we cannot imagine life without organizations.

The French are credited with introducing the concept of bureaucracy in the eighteenth century, setting the stage for the growth of modern large-scale organizations. Basic functions were standardized, based on policies and prescribed operating rules. An executive made decisions and set the direction for an enterprise, but responsibility for carrying out the work was delegated to staff. Bureaucracy has become a hallmark of all sectors of modern society. Industrialization and the modern economy depend on this organizing principle.

There is a downside to modern organization, as many studies show. It tends to be dehumanizing. Yet all sectors of life in contemporary society depend on this model. So how can we cultivate a spirituality that transforms such an environment?

The Scriptures do not give us a single clue as to how to run a board of directors, a program commission, or a committee. The concepts of the CEO, a board of directors, and stakeholders are absent from the Bible. All of this belongs to the modern period; they have become powerful cultural symbols. How do we bridge between Christian faith and contemporary culture?

The theme of spiritual gifts took on new importance for me when I read Hans Küng's book *The Church*.[5] By the 1960s Küng was a rising Roman Catholic theological star. Brilliant and articulate, he had been a consultant at Vatican II and was a champion for renewal of the church. He did not hide his impatience with the heavy weight of traditionalism and the tight control exercised by the church's hierarchy. Küng saw the Catholic Church as tied to the past, not oriented toward the future.

In this book, Küng appealed to the New Testament vision of the church. A defining dimension of this vision is that the church is a body in which every member is intended to play an active role. Küng had no patience with the traditional division between clergy and laity, between the passive silent majority and the powerful hierarchy. Paul's vision of the church starts at a different point. He focuses on the church as an interdependent whole organism. To be sustained, every part must be in place and working properly. Preserving the dignity and integrity of each member is essential to the well-being and fruitfulness of the whole.

The Holy Spirit bestows on each member of the body of Christ a "grace-gift" (Greek, *charisma*; plural, *charismata*). Every member of the body is a bearer of Spirit-given grace. No one can be a member apart from grace. While this grace-gift is given to the individual as a token of the Spirit's presence, these grace-gifts are not a personal possession for personal satisfaction. Each gift is held in trust and is to be exercised on behalf of the entire body.

Paul paints a richly textured picture of life in the body as one in which each believer plays an indispensable role on behalf of the whole. He describes the body as an organism of great complexity, which can be sustained only by respecting the interdependence among all its parts. To describe how an organization is to work, Paul's vision challenges us to think outside the box of administrative charts that depend on job descriptions and lines of accountability. Repeatedly I have observed that the most effective Christian ministry takes place when an individual's grace-gift is recognized and honored.

—Wilbert R. Shenk of Elkhart, Indiana, has served as senior professor of mission history and contemporary culture at Fuller School of Intercultural Studies.

Maintaining Priorities in a Nano World

> I press on to take hold of that for which Christ Jesus took
> hold of me.
>
> —Paul, in Philippians 3:12b NIV

All human groups—whether family, company, local congregation, or tennis club—necessarily develop their own particular culture. A group's culture is what enables it to survive in its environment. Without a culture, there will be chaos and dysfunction.

Over time, cultures must change because the environment is dynamic, not static. A culture that does not adapt will not survive. Even cultures that resist wholesale adaptation to the larger society must devise adaptive mechanisms in order to cope.

Even though it is seldom put in these terms, a good deal of a board of directors' energy is expended on negotiating adjustments between an organization and the changing environment: mandated regulations, financial challenges, personnel issues, and concerns raised by an organization's supporting constituency. An agency devoted to Christian ministry ought to lead the way in modeling a corporate culture that combines the highest professional standards with sterling Christian values. It should also demonstrate effective interaction with its culture. This has become a tall order in contemporary culture, with its unprecedented fast pace of change.

In 1986 Eric Drexler published *Engines of Creation: The Coming Era of Nanotechnology*.[6] Drexler promoted the technological potential of nanoscale phenomena (measured by the nanometer = one billionth of a meter). The development of nanotechnology the past twenty-five years has been an exploding frontier. Rather than slowing the pace of culture, it has only accelerated it.

We often get the feeling that we are being upstaged and outpaced by our culture. The temptation is to surrender to these powers. But if we do so, we lose perspective on who we are and what our true purpose is. This applies both to individuals as well as boards, committees, and commissions. If we are to live purposefully in a nanoworld, we need to cultivate and maintain a clear perspective on who we are and what our life purpose is.

The hymn "The Work Is Thine, O Christ" furnishes a framework that will guide us when we need to establish our whereabouts:[7] (1) Jesus Christ is Master; (2) regardless of our position in a cultural system, we are never more than servants or less than servants; and (3) although our environment changes continually, we always find our bearings by remembering this order of priority.

The apostle Paul understood the way we cling tightly to our ambitions. He describes discipleship as a process of being emptied of self and filled with God until we can say with Paul, "Christ lives in me" (Gal 2:20 NIV). We can never fulfill our God-given vocation so long as we hold on to our own ambitions and goals. Discipleship cannot be separated from self-sacrifice and wholehearted surrender to God. Dietrich Bonhoeffer spoke of the "cost of discipleship," driving home the point that genuine discipleship is always life lived on God's terms, not our own.[8] Discipleship requires willing submission on the part of the servant to the master. In the kingdom of God our high calling is to be servants. All—individuals, board members, executives, field workers—stand under the lordship of Jesus Christ, the one who was the Suffering Servant.

—Wilbert R. Shenk of Elkhart, Indiana, has served as senior professor of mission history and contemporary culture at Fuller School of Intercultural Studies.

The Legacy We Leave Behind

> The good leave an inheritance for their children's children.
> —Proverbs 13:22 NIV

Each birthday is a celebration when we are young. We really are getting to be grown up. Even half years are noticed. Somewhere along the way, the thrill diminishes. By our late thirties, we may even hate to see birthdays approaching. For many, this continues until they approach the century mark, then birthdays again become celebrations of accomplishment. "I'm ninety-six-and-a-half," someone will say with obvious pride.

A few years ago I began to look at birthdays not with regret but with gratitude. In a world where so many never see their fiftieth year, birthdays are really a cause to celebrate. I've begun to realize that we're not entitled to anything, and life is short.

This has triggered something else in my awareness. I find myself thinking more about what I'll leave behind when my heavenly summons comes. Proverbs 13:22 says, "The good leave an inheritance for their children's children." When I die, I may not have all that much to leave my children or grandchildren in terms of this world's goods. However the Paris Hiltons and Lisa Marie Presleys of this world bear witness that inheritances measured in dollars are often more of a curse than a blessing.

There is a legacy we *can* leave to those who follow us that blesses beyond measure. That is a spiritual legacy: a life lived according to godly values, a modeling of kingdom priorities, a demonstration of passionate and joyful commitment to the things of God. That foundation gives purpose and meaning to everything, from the most mundane task to the big-picture discussions in the boardroom. It is the worthy inheritance we can leave to our descendants. And won't that serve them much better than things that might distract their attention from God or lessen their dependence on God?

On the day I leave this world, I want to feel content in knowing that I have fulfilled God's calling on my life and thus have made a difference for eternity in the niche where God has placed me. No, I'm not going to leave behind a legacy like Billy Graham's: God has not called me to be Billy Graham. I'm not going to leave behind a legacy like that of other saints we might name, beside whose earthly kingdom accomplishments my own pale by comparison. But God has not called me to their spot, to their role, to their place. God has not needed me there: God needs me where I am.

I want to fulfill God's calling on my life, making a difference for eternity in the niche where God has needed me to serve. If those who gather to bid me farewell are clear on why I have tried to live as I have, and if I have accurately reflected how precious Jesus has been and is to me in that journey, and if I have instilled in them at least the seeds of yearning to live their own lives for God's glory, bent on fulfilling his calling for them—then I think I will have succeeded in leaving behind a wonderful inheritance, for generations to come.

Again the Proverb says, "The good leave an inheritance for their children's children." What you do now determines what you will leave behind. Think about it.

—Joe N. Sherer of Mount Joy, Pennsylvania, is a pastor and board chair of Eastern Mennonite Missions, Salunga, Pennsylvania.

Listening for the Voice of God

> David inquired of the LORD.
> —1 Samuel 30:8

The search committee had spoken, but I wavered. Should I step from the comfort of a ministry I loved into another that tugs at my deepest motivations but involves considerable risk? How can I, how can we, know how God is leading? Counsel was mixed, my heart was torn.

We decided to call together a small group of key leaders from each of the two organizations involved in the decision and invite their counsel, hoping to reach a common consensus. I agreed to accept their decision.

We retreated to a neutral location. This group had never met before. It would almost certainly never meet again. I respected all of them and was confident that the Holy Spirit would lead us to a good consensus. There was no contention in the meeting. We counseled, prayed, and shared our hearts. Everyone listened well before recessing for the night, anticipating that in the morning the answer would be clear and unanimous.

It did not happen. One side said "stay," the other said "come." There were no crossovers, no breaking of ranks. In the end all eyes turned to me: "The decision is yours."

I was disappointed. Was it expecting too much that a group of godly leaders would help me with my life-altering decision? Must we make these decisions ourselves? Later I came to understand that each group did not feel commissioned to reverse a decision arrived at with others. My expectations had been unrealistic. What now?

Gradually I came to see the meeting in a new way. Rather than anticipating a quick consensus, it was a time to listen for God's voice among the symphony of human voices. God was indeed speaking through men and women of faith. They were honoring both God and me by refusing to cobble together a hasty, shallow "consensus." They had opened their hearts and spoken transparently, giving all of us, especially my wife and me, the opportunity to listen and respond to each other and sense God's leading.

We digested what we had heard. Lingering in our memories were the words of the elder statesman from the inviting organization: "When I was invited to serve on this search committee, I had no idea whom to suggest for this leadership role. So I prayed. Then one night I was awakened with an insistent thought. It was your name. It was strange to me, and at first I tried to repress it, for I knew you were busily engaged, and I had no reason to think you were available. But it wouldn't go away. So I brought it to the search committee, and here we are."

With that word and others like it, I accepted the position peacefully and with conviction. God had indeed spoken, though not as I had imagined. This experience encourages boards to listen intently, persistently, and confidently for God's voice in all decisions facing them. With Samuel we say, "Speak, Lord, for your servants are listening" (cf. 1 Sam 3:10).

—Richard Showalter, Landisville, Pennsylvania, has served as president and CEO of Eastern Mennonite Missions, Salunga, Pennsylvania. He is chair of the mission commission of Mennonite World Conference, author of *On the Way with Jesus,* and coauthor with his wife, Jewel, of *Silk Road Pilgrimage: Discovering the Church of the East.*

The Board's Twofold Challenge

Follow the way of love and eagerly desire gifts of the Spirit, especially prophecy.

—Paul, in 1 Corinthians 14:1 NIV

For something great to happen, there must be a great dream. Behind every great achievement is a dreamer of great dreams.

—Robert K. Greenleaf[9]

I have spent the past thirty years as a nonprofit executive, working with board trustees, and I have served on boards myself. I have witnessed and felt two great challenges that come with serving on boards.

First is the tendency of boards to focus on operational matters when what is most needed is a greater vision (dreaming great dreams). Second is a tendency to view the volunteer task of fundraising as an unhappy chore. As a result most don't do it well, even though fundraising can be a profound spiritual act of inviting others into a shared sense of commitment and community.

Trustees as servant leaders seek to nurture their abilities to dream great dreams, to conceptualize. Dreaming requires them to concentrate their attention beyond day-to-day realities. This requires discipline and practice.

In my experience, the art of conceptualization is best practiced when grounded in what Quakers call "that of God in everyone." And it is that combination of vision and spirit that can take an organization far.

The board's second challenge is to rise to the spirituality of fundraising, the need for which is illustrated in the following traditional story.

For want of a nail, the shoe was lost;
For want of the shoe, the horse was lost;
For want of the horse, the rider was lost;
For want of the rider, the battle was lost;
For want of the battle, the kingdom was lost;
And all for the want of a nail.[10]

The point of this parable is that the smallest of absences can create the largest of losses in unexpected ways. Because the initial absence (the nail) is inextricably linked to a subsequent chain of events—each of which is larger and more problematic than the previous event—it becomes ever more difficult in hindsight to recognize the earliest leverage point. And so the kingdom is lost, when it might have been saved by the smallest of differences early on.

If we think about it, most of us hold in our pockets the "nails" (either treasure or time) that can help to ensure that the organizations we hold in trust for others shall not perish. Yet, much like the nail in that story, we sometimes fail to foresee what impact our lack of support may have in the world. That is why it is helpful to frame our understanding of fundraising and philanthropy along the lines of what Henri Nouwen has called "a spirituality of fundraising." "Fundraising," says Nouwen, "is proclaiming what we believe in such a way that we offer other people an opportunity to participate with us in our vision and mission."[11]

The idea of trustees as servant leaders, those who see their calling to board service as a combination of dreaming great dreams and helping to make those dreams become real through inspirited fundraising, is for me a profound expression of spirituality in the boardroom.

—Larry C. Spears of Indianapolis, Indiana, is author of a dozen books on servant leadership. From 1990–2007 he served as president and CEO of the Greenleaf Center. Since 2008 he has served as president and CEO of the Spears Center for Servant Leadership.

Freedom Through Self-Emptying

> Let this same mind be in you that was in Christ Jesus,
>> who, though he was in the form of God,
>>> did not regard equality with God as something to be
>>>> exploited,
>> but emptied himself.
>
> —Paul, in Philippians 2:5-7a

Christ chose not to cling to his prerogative to be God in his very nature, but out of his love for God, he was completely consumed to do God's will; to be the means of redeeming the created order.

My wife and I are transitioning from 3,000 square feet of living space to a 1,200-square-foot cottage in a retirement village. We are emptying closets, drawers, and filing cabinets of things that have accumulated over almost fifty years. As we do so, we are reminded of spiritual and mental clutter. Perhaps the physical emptying makes our spiritual emptying easier!

Christ's choice to empty himself resulted from his great love for God, a love that God had also shed on him (John 17). Because of such transcending love, Jesus desired always to "will one thing" (Kierkegaard): the glory of God and God's kingdom.

Our human, narcissistic, ego-driven choice is a great threat to life and peace in our Western world. The grasping for personal power, wealth, status, and prestige always undermines the flourishing human spirit that God intends. We cry out with the apostle Paul, "Who will rescue me from this body of death?" (Rom 7:24). Our answer is found in Jesus.

Christ shows us the way to freedom from bondage to self by prayerfulness. Jesus used prayer for centering to face the challenges of his day. He addressed God with the Aramaic word "Abba." An alternative centering prayer word taught by a spiritual master is to "let go." In her book *Psalms for Praying*, Nan C. Merrill often uses the word *abandon*. Abandon yourself to God![12]

Freedom comes by dwelling with Scriptures that focus on God's love for us: Read Isaiah 43:1-4a and insert your own name in place of Israel. Or read John 17:24, 26: "Father, I desire that those also, whom you have given me, may be with me where I am, . . . so that the love with which you have loved me may be in them, and I in them."

Freedom comes by reading the stories of people who have succeeded in freeing themselves from the domination of self, such as Mother Teresa, Dietrich Bonhoeffer, and John Woolman. Freedom comes by keeping a journal of where we have succeeded in getting it right, together with notation of thanksgiving and also where we "blew it" and where we need God's grace for tomorrow.

Freedom comes by committing ourselves to doing one little random act of love each day for someone—preferably someone who can't return the favor.

In all, we want to seek the mind of Christ, who showed us the way to be emptied of an ego-motivated self and full of joy in doing that which brings happiness to others.

—A. Richard Weaver, Lititz, Pennsylvania, has served as a missionary physician and as a spiritual director and retreat leader with Kairos School of Spiritual Formation.

Rooted and Grounded in Love

> I pray that, according to the riches of his glory, he may
> grant that you may be strengthened in your inner being
> with power through his Spirit, and that Christ may dwell
> in your hearts through faith, as you are being rooted and
> grounded in love.
> —Paul, in Ephesians 3:16-17

A mighty wind blew through on New Year's Eve, with gusts of up to sixty miles per hour. As the wind wailed in the window, I couldn't help but look at the roof and wonder, "How viable is this thing, really?" The wind whipped up whatever was loose and adrift, scouring dry leaves and debris across the ground as if saying, "Out with the old, in with the new."

Meanwhile the huge trees swayed, rooted and grounded, stately in their majestic grace! So tall. So firm. Yet able to bend with ease, yielding to the wind. Rooted and grounded.

Paul's prayer for his beloved Ephesian brothers and sisters is powerful in its beauty—a prayer he likely wrote while sitting in prison in Rome: may you be strengthened in your inner being, rooted and grounded in love.

Mystics remind us that everything is connected to everything else. Beneath the broken surface of our lives, says Thomas Merton, there remains "a hidden wholeness." Our roots are held in a web of connection, of relationship, of love—strengthened by the power of the Spirit—even as the gusts scour debris from the surface.

And it is that deep connection, our firm grounding in loving community and in the Spirit, that makes it possible to bend, to yield to the call of God to new places.

No one is more surprised than I am that I decided to rise to the challenge of a new job. For months I knew there was no way I would move and gave loud assertions to close family and friends. "It is far too costly," I said. "All the stars will have to line up," I said (whatever that means), and I could see no way that they would. But I've never felt so inexorably led . . . step by step . . . to yield.

I'm an early riser, often up before daybreak. During the months leading up to the decision, I could hardly wait to get to the candle and prayer books, holding on for dear life. The ground was shifting beneath me; the wind was threatening to tear the roof off.

Walter Brueggemann writes in *Awed to Heaven, Rooted in Earth*:

> We yield because you, beyond us, are our God
> We are your creatures, met by your holiness,
>   by your holiness made our true selves.
> And we yield.[13]

I don't yield easily. I resist doing anything out of a sense of obligation or an imposed ideological dutifulness.

But I come alive to Paul's elemental rootage: "I pray that you may have the power to comprehend, with all the saints, what is the breadth and length and height and depth, and to know the love of Christ that surpasses knowledge, so that you may be filled with all the fullness of God" (Eph 3:18-19).

For me, prayer is mostly about staying rooted and grounded in love—the wellspring of joy; the freedom to bend, even to yield. The grace to come alive to God's call.

—Sara Wenger Shenk is president of Associated Mennonite Biblical Seminary, Elkhart, Indiana. She is author of *Thank You for Asking: Conversing with Young Adults about the Future Church* (2005) and *Anabaptist Ways of Knowing: A Conversation about Tradition-Based Critical Education* (2003).

Prayers

God of inexhaustible mystery,
    of unfathomable creativity,
    of deep wells of wisdom,
you honor us by calling us into relationship with you.
You seek communion with all the creatures you have made.
You promise that if we need wisdom, we can ask and receive.

In response to such generosity,
    our hearts overflow in praise.
Especially today we are thankful for the many gifts we have received
    from your hand ...
[*Invite board members to offer free prayers of thanks.*]

We confess that at times we are reluctant to respond
    to your call to communion.
We fear intimacy and hesitate to draw near to you.
Forgive us for the ways we neglect your invitation
    or turn away from you.
[*Invite board members to offer prayers of confession, both personal and corporate.*]

We are keenly aware of the limits of our knowledge
    and our need for the wisdom that is from above.
Especially today we seek your guidance for the decisions we face
    and for the gift of vision to see and know your desires
    for the work we do.
[*Invite board members to offer prayers of petition and intercession.*]

God, who is beyond all we can imagine,
    we are grateful that you dwell among us and within us.
Fill us today with your gracious Spirit.
Let the work we do reflect your wisdom
    and bring honor to you both now and forever.

We pray in the name of Jesus,
>   the One who reveals your hidden mysteries. Amen.

—Marlene Kropf is associate professor of spiritual formation and worship, Associated Mennonite Biblical Seminary, and the former denominational minister of worship for Mennonite Church USA.

[*Place hands on table, palms up.*]

Sustaining God,
>   We open ourselves to new insights, new strength, and new hope.
>   We open our minds to wisdom, imagination, creativity.
>   We open our spirits to transformation, compassion, grace.
Empowering God,
>   Grant this board the fullness of your Spirit.
>   Grant our staff the eagerness to lead.
>   Grant our constituency the commitment to accomplish our
>   corporate goals.
Loving God,
>   Bless this emerging hope for faithfulness.
>   Bless our deep discernment.
>   Bless our growth in vision and spiritual maturity.
Amen.

—Dorothy Nickel Friesen has spent her professional career in the English classroom as teacher and the last twenty-eight years as a Mennonite pastor, seminary administrator, and conference minister.

God of heaven and earth, you dare us to reach for wisdom that comes from above, for that which is most pure. Too often, as Paul of old, we see through a glass, darkly. We ask you to illumine us, to inspire us, to brighten our path so that we might truly see thee more clearly even as we follow thee more nearly and love thee more dearly. Amen.

—David Johnson Rowe is copastor of Greenfield Hill Congregational Church, Fairfield, Connecticut.

Notes

Chapter 1: Discovering Spirituality

1. See http://theotherpages.org/poems/books/tennyson/tennyson01.html.

2. Robert K. Greenleaf, *Servant Leadership: A Journey into the Nature of Legitimate Power and Greatness* (Mahwah, NJ: Paulist Press, 1977), 35.

3. Eric Klein and John B. Izzo, *Awakening Corporate Soul: Four Paths to Unleash the Power of People at Work* (Lions Bay, BC: Fairwinds Press, 1997).

4. William A. Guillory, *The Living Organization: Spirituality in the Workplace* (Salt Lake City: Innovations International, 1997).

5. See http://www.seeingthingswhole.org/PDF/STW-toward-theology-of-institutions.pdf.

Chapter 2: Moving Spirituality

1. Samuel Preiswerk, "The Work Is Thine," in *Hymnal: A Worship Book* (Scottdale, PA: Herald Press, 1992), 396.

2. Walter Wink, *Engaging the Powers* (Minneapolis: Augsburg Fortress, 1992).

3. Ekhart Tolle, *A New Earth: Awakening to your Life's Purpose* (New York: Plume/Penguin Group, 2005).

4. Roland Rolheiser, *The Shattered Lantern: Rediscovering a Felt Presence of God*, rev. ed. (New York: Crossroad, 2001).

5. William A. Guillory, *The Living Organization-Spirituality in the Workplace* (Salt Lake City: Innovations International, 1997).

6. Parker J. Palmer, *Leading from Within* (Washington, DC: Servant Leadership School, 1990), 20.

Chapter 3: Achieving Spirituality

1. Theodore Roethke, "In a Dark Time," *The Collected Poems of Theodore Roethke* (Garden City, NY: Anchor, 1975).

2. Thérèse Lisieux, *Story of a Soul: The Autobiography of St. Thérèse of Lisieux* (Washington, DC: ICS Publications, 1996), 242.

3. Walter Wink, *Engaging the Powers* (Minneapolis: Augsburg Fortress, 1992).

4. Richard J. Foster, *Prayer: Finding the Heart's True Home* (San Francisco: HarperOne, 1992), 247.

5. William W. How, "We Give Thee but Thine Own," in *Hymnal: A Worship Book* (Scottdale, PA: Herald Press, 1992), 384.

6. Roland Rolheiser, *The Shattered Lantern: Rediscovering a Felt Presence of God* (New York: Crossroad, 2001).

7. Brother Lawrence, *The Practice of the Presence of God: The Original 17th-Century Letters and Conversations of Brother Lawrence* (Cincinnati: Forward Movement Publications, 2007).

8. Parker J. Palmer, *Let Your Life Speak: Listen for the Voice of Vocation* (San Francisco: Jossey-Bass, 2000), 7.

Chapter 4: Living Spirituality

1. A few examples: Jesus' baptism: "This is my Son, the Beloved, with whom I am well pleased" (Matt 3:17); tempted in the wilderness: "Then the devil left him, and suddenly angels came and waited on him" (Matt 4:11); Jesus' transfiguration: "This is my Son, my Chosen; listen to him" (Luke 9:35); in Gethsemane: "An angel from heaven appeared to him and gave him strength" (Luke 22:43); on the cross: "Father, into your hands I commend my spirit" (Luke 23:46); ascended: "The Lord Jesus . . . was taken up into heaven and sat down at the right hand of God" (Mark 16:19).

2. C. Norman Kraus, *The Authentic Witness: Credibility and Authority* (Grand Rapids: Eerdmans, 1999), alt.

3. Robert Browning, a line from "Andrea del Sarto," in *Men and Women* (London: Chapman & Hall, 1855).

4. Edgar Stoesz, *Doing Good Even Better: How to Be an Effective Board Member of a Nonprofit Organization* (Intercourse, PA: Good Books, 2007); John Carver and Miriam Carver, *Reinventing Your Board: A Step-by-Step Guide to Implementing Policy Governance*, 2nd ed. (San Francisco: John Wiley, 2006); John Carver, *Boards That Make a Difference: A New Design for Leadership in Nonprofit and Public Organizations*, 3rd ed. (San Francisco: Jossey-Bass, 2006).

5. David Young, *Springs of Living Water* (Scottdale, PA: Herald Press, 2008).

Chapter 6: Meditations When Faced with Major Disappointments

1. Henri J. M. Nouwen, *Bread for the Journey* (New York: HarperCollins, 1997), January 12.
2. Max De Pree, *Leadership Jazz* (New York: Dell, 1993), 57.
3. John of the Cross, *The Dark Night of the Soul* (Spanish original, 16th century), available in various translations and editions, such as the 3rd rev. ed., trans. and ed. E. Allison Peers (Garden City, NY: Image Books, 1959), http://www.ccel.org/ccel/john_cross/dark_night.toc.html.
4. Anna L. Barbauld, "Lord, Should Rising Whirlwinds," in *Hymnal: A Worship Book* (Scottdale, PA: Herald Press, 1992), 92.

Chapter 7: Meditations When Contemplating a Major Decision

1. Robert K. Greenleaf, *Servant Leadership: A Journey into the Nature of Legitimate Power and Greatness* (Mahwah, NJ: Paulist Press, 1977), 35.
2. Henry T. Blackaby and Claude V. King, *Experiencing God: Knowing and Doing the Will of God* (Nashville: LifeWay Press, 1990), 109.
3. Søren Kierkegaard, *Journals and Papers*, ed. and trans. Howard V. Hong and Edna H. Hong, vol. 1, A–E (1843; Bloomington: Indiana University Press, 1967).
4. Louis E. Boone, 1941–2005, American academic writer on business, coauthor with David L. Kurtz of *Contemporary Business* (Hinsdale, IL: Dryden Press, 1976, plus many later editions). Cf. John Greenleaf Whittier, "For of all sad words of tongue or pen, the saddest are these: 'It might have been!'" in *Maud Muller* (1856), stanza 53.
5. Frederick Buechner, in *Wishful Thinking: A Seeker's ABC* (San Francisco: HarperSanFrancisco, 1993), 119: "The place God calls you to, is the place where your deep gladness and the world's deep need meet."
6. From the poem "Dreams" (1926), by Langston Hughes, in *The Collected Poems of Langston Hughes*, ed. Arnold Rampersad and David Roessel (New York: Knopf/Random House, 1994).
7. Gloria Gaither, "Gentle Shepherd, Come and Lead Us," in *Hymnal: A Worship Book* (Scottdale, PA: Herald Press, 1992), 352.

Chapter 8: Meditations When Conflict Threatens Board Unity

1. John Paul Lederach, *The Little Book of Conflict Transformation* (Intercourse, PA: Good Books, 2003); Eckhart Tolle, *A New Earth: Awakening to Your Life's Purpose* (New York: Dutton/Penguin Group, 2005).

2. "Holy God, We Praise Thy Name," from "Te Deum Laudamus," trans. Ignaz Franz, in *Hymnal: A Worship Book* (Scottdale, PA: Herald Press, 1992), 121.

Chapter 9: Meditations for Ordinary Times

1. John W. Gardner, *No Easy Victories* (New York: Harper & Row, 1968), 40.

2. Stephen R. Covey, *Seven Habits of Highly Effective People* (New York: Simon & Schuster, 1989), Habit 3; this book led to many editions and spin-offs.

3. As in Stephen R. Covey, *The Eighth Habit: From Effectiveness to Greatness* (New York: Free Press, 2005), 160.

4. Wendell Berry, *A Place on Earth* (New York: Harcourt, Brace & World, 1967; revised, San Francisco: North Point Press, 1983).

5. Frederick Buechner, *Now and Then: A Memoir of Vocation* (New York: HarperCollins, 1983), 93.

6. "CTIA–The Wireless Association® Announces Semi-Annual Wireless Industry Survey Results," http://www.ctia.org/media/press/body.cfm/prid/1936.

7. T. S. Eliot, "Ash-Wednesday," in *Collected Poems, 1909–1962* (London: Faber & Faber, 1963), http://www.msgr.ca/msgr-7/ash_wednesday_t_s_eliot.htm.

8. Kathleen Norris, *Amazing Grace: A Vocabulary of Faith* (New York: Riverhead Books, 1998), 141.

9. Desmond Tutu, *Made for Goodness and Why This Makes All the Difference* (San Francisco: HarperOne, 2010), Kindle ed.

10. Janet K. Ruffing, "Resisting the Demon of Busyness," *Spiritual Life*, Summer 1996.

Chapter 10: Meditations to Seek Wisdom and a Deeper Spirituality

1. Dorothy Sayers, *Letters to a Diminished Church: Passionate Arguments for the Relevance of Christian Doctrine* (Nashville:

W Publishing Group, 2004), http://www.faith-at-work.net/Docs/WhyWork.pdf.

2. Stephen M. R. Covey, with Rebecca R. Merrill, *The Speed of Trust: The One Thing That Changes Everything* (New York: Free Press, 2006).

3. J. Philip Newell, *Celtic Prayers from Iona* (New York: Paulist Press, 1997); idem, *Celtic Benediction: Morning and Night Prayer* (Grand Rapids: Eerdmans, 2000).

4. Cf. David Starr Jordan, *The Philosophy of Hope*, 2nd ed. (New York: P. Elder, 1907).

5. Hans Küng, *The Church*, trans. from German by Ray and Rosaleen Ockenden (London, Burns & Oates, 1967).

6. K. Eric Drexler, *Engines of Creation: The Coming Era of Nanotechnology* (Garden City, NY: Anchor/Doubleday, 1986).

7. Samuel Preiswerk, "The Work Is Thine," in *Hymnal: A Worship Book* (Scottdale, PA: Herald Press, 1992), 396.

8. Dietrich Bonhoeffer, *The Cost of Discipleship*, trans. R. H. Fuller (London: SCM, 1948).

9. Robert K. Greenleaf, *Servant Leadership: A Journey into the Nature of Legitimate Power and Greatness* (Mahwah, NJ: Paulist Press, 1977).

10. Cf. George Herbert, in Jacula Prudentum (1651), no. 499; Benjamin Franklin, *Poor Richard's Almanac* (1758), "Preface: Courteous Reader."

11. Henri Nouwen, *A Spirituality of Fundraising* (Nashville: Upper Room Books, 2011).

12. Nan C. Merrill, *Psalms for Praying: An Invitation to Wholeness* (New York: Continuum, 1996).

13. Walter Brueggemann, *Awed to Heaven, Rooted in Earth: Prayers by Walter Brueggemann*, ed. Edwin Searcy (Minneapolis: Augsburg Fortress, 2003), 3.

For Further Reading

While the focus of this book is on spirituality in the boardroom, we acknowledge that spirituality originates in those who occupy the boardroom. From the many good books on personal spirituality, we have selected several that we found to be especially helpful.

Ruth Haley Barton. *Strengthening the Soul of Your Leadership: Seeking God in the Crucible of Ministry*. Downers Grove, IL: InterVarsity Press, 2008.
Ruth Haley Barton invites readers to an honest exploration of what happens when leaders lose track of their souls. The book weaves together contemporary illustrations with penetrating insights from the life of Moses.

Each of the thirteen chapters is introduced with a Bible quotation featuring the life and leadership style of Moses; each concludes with an exercise that provides practical application.

According to Barton, leaders who have grown and developed their souls are continually seeking God. Even amid leadership demands, the focus on seeking God helps these leaders remain faithful to God's call and maintain their commitment to ministry throughout their lives.

Margaret Benefiel. *The Soul of a Leader: Finding Your Path to Fulfillment and Success*. New York: Crossroad, 2008.
This book is divided into three parts, each of which comprises three chapters. The message in each of the nine chapters is built on real-life experiences, giving the book both a practical and a theoretical message. That message is focused on the soul of the leader.

Benefiel gently reminds leaders that the health and success of an organization depends on their ongoing tending of their own spiritual growth and needs. Putting this off can leave the leader depleted when the organization needs strength. Spiritual growth can be found through religious faith, or it can be expressed through other means.

Juana Bordas. *Salsa, Soul, and Spirit: Leadership for a Multicultural Age.* San Francisco: Berrett-Koehler, 2007.
Juana Bordas asserts that leadership in a complex and connected world requires multicultural competence. She offers succinct descriptions of traditional Latino, African American, and American Indian cultures and identifies eight characteristics of leadership and organization that are common to all three.

Bordas illustrates the eight characteristics with the stories of leaders from within each of the cultures. The author contends that these principles are critical to competent leadership in an increasingly multicultural world. Bordas's work is an important contribution to the literature of leadership in North America, which has primarily reflected Anglo and dominant cultural perspectives.

Jay A. Conger, comp. *Spirit at Work: Discovering the Spirituality in Leadership.* San Francisco: Jossey-Bass, 1994.
Jay Conger offers insights into the nature of spirituality and leadership through the contributions of Parker Palmer, Katherine Tyler Scott, Brian McDermott, SJ, and others. As Conger notes in the preface, "This book is about the search for shared ground among leadership, the workforce, and spirituality" (xiii). The book takes the treatment of leadership beyond a focus on the products or results of leadership to more carefully examine how the inner spiritual dimensions of the leader influence leadership and organizational life.

The contributors represent a diverse range of faiths and worldviews, and each author explores the interface of spirituality and the pragmatic dimensions of organizational life. For example, Scott addresses the challenge of conflict and reconciliation; McDermott offers suggestions on how the principles of Ignatian spirituality can shape the leadership of groups; Rabindra Kanungo and Manuel Mendonca reflect on how spirituality and deep moral grounding shape the use of power within an organization. Though published nearly twenty years ago, this book offers provocative insight into leadership, spirituality, and organizational life.

Meditations by Author

The Authors

Edgar Stoesz has spent his entire life in a variety of for-profit and nonprofit organizations, most of them in a faith tradition. He has written ten books, five of which are related to board work, and has addressed hundreds of organizations on good board service practices and techniques.

In addition to serving thirty-four years with Mennonite Central Committee, Edgar served on and chaired the boards of Habitat for Humanity International, American Leprosy Missions, Heifer International, and Hospital Albert Schweitzer (Haiti). In addition, Edgar served as moderator of Atlantic Coast Conference, part of Mennonite Church USA.

Edgar's wife of fifty-six years, Gladys, died while this book was in process. Both were born and grew up in Mountain Lake, Minnesota, then moved to Akron, Pennsylvania, in 1956, where Edgar continues to live. He has four grown children and seven grandchildren.

Rick M. Stiffney serves as President/CEO of Mennonite Health Services Alliance, which represents seventy-one not-for-profit providers, including community mental-health organizations, some acute care systems, developmental disabilities providers, and numerous nursing homes and retirement communities.

Rick has worked for over twenty-five years in various health and human service leadership capacities. He consults broadly

289

across the not-for-profit sector, with special attention to work with governing boards and CEOs.

Currently Rick chairs the board of Goshen College, Goshen, Indiana, and has served on numerous nonprofit boards. Rick was a cofounder of the national Inter-faith Roundtable, a national consortium of faith-based associations that serve health and human service organizations.

Rick is a member of Berkey Avenue Mennonite Fellowship, Goshen, Indiana, and chairs the governing board. He was born in Kendallville, Indiana, and now resides in Goshen with his wife, Kathy. They have two grown children, Ryan and Kristin, and two grandchildren, Ben and Thomas. His hobbies are aerobic exercise, golf, and landscaping.

We acknowledge the funding support of these
organizations, with gratitude for their commitment
to spiritually grounded governance.

Goodville Mutual Casualty Company
Brook Lane
Living Branches
Mennonite Home Communities
Penn Foundation
Rockhill Mennonite Community
Landis Homes
Mennonite Village
Thurston Woods Village